GRAMBO

The True Adventures of an
American Grandmother in Baghdad

. . . and Beyond

Evelyn Dykes Chriswell

WestBow
PRESS

A DIVISION OF THOMAS NELSON

ISBN: 978-1-4497-0542-8 (sc)
ISBN: 978-1-4497-0544-2 (hc)
ISBN: 978-1-4497-0543-5 (e)

WestBow Press books may be ordered through booksellers or by contacting:

WestBow Press
A Division of Thomas Nelson
1663 Liberty Drive
Bloomington, IN 47403
www.westbowpress.com
1-(866) 928-1240

Because of the dynamic nature of the Internet, any Web addresses or links contained in this book may have changed since publication and may no longer be valid. The views expressed in this work are solely those of the author and do not necessarily reflect the views of the publisher, and the publisher hereby disclaims any responsibility for them.

In some incidents, names and identifying characteristics of people have been altered.

Unless otherwise noted, scripture is taken from the HOLY BIBLE, NEW INTERNATIONAL VERSION®. Copyright © 1973, 1978, 1984 Biblica. Used by permission of Zondervan. All rights reserved.

Library of Congress Control Number: 2010935773

Printed in the United States of America

WestBow Press rev. date: 12/08/2010

In Memory of My Mother

Agnes Hope McKellar Webb

Whose quiet voice still gently encourages
me to be all God wants me to be

Dedicated to My Father
P.V. Webb

A man of great character and discipline who
truly loves God, church, and family

For

The soldiers and contractors who have given their lives
in service to their Country, so that all of us can enjoy
the freedoms on which this nation is based

Special Thanks
To my family and forever friends, without whose love and
encouragement I would not have been able to complete this book. You
have rejoiced with me and cried with me through all my peaks and
valleys of life, and I thank God every day for each and every one of you
Grace, mercy, and peace to you all

Evelyn Chriswell

"Many, oh Lord are the wonders you have done…
were I to speak and tell of them, they would be too many to declare."

Psalms 40:5 NIV

Table of Contents

INTRODUCTION

Grambo Is on a Mission!

My life has been a rich tapestry of triumph and tragedy.

I've experienced the joy of bringing precious children into the world, as well as the heartbreak of saying goodbye to the men I've loved. I've journeyed to the ends of the Earth and have walked in the footsteps of my Lord and Savior, Jesus Christ.

I've gripped the hands of countless people, praying for their salvation. I've comforted the elderly, wiped the tears of unwed moms, and encouraged young soldiers in the heat of battle.

I'm a Christian woman, a sister, a mentor, a musician, a pastor's wife, a parent, a grandmother, a diehard over-comer . . . and a military missionary!

I am *Grambo.*

At a time when many my age were counting down to the much-deserved peace of retirement, I decided to pull on a pair of army boots and head off to the turmoil of war. In October 2004, at age sixty-three, I began a new chapter of my life as a civilian Morale, Welfare, and Recreation (MWR) contractor. For three unforgettable years, I served proudly alongside United States and coalition forces at Camp Victory in Baghdad, Iraq.

I've walked in the halls of opulent palaces that were once used for evil, but are now ground zero for freedom. I've celebrated victories with the troops and have cried over their losses. I've befriended the Iraqi people, and I've endured lonely moments in dark bunkers.

So, why did I do it? Why would a proper Southern lady uproot her sane life in Louisiana and journey seven-thousand-miles into danger, especially at my age?

My answer—which will unfold in these pages—boils down to one simple, yet amazingly profound truth: *God is in control of my life.*

I believe He placed me right where He wanted me. The Lord worked in my heart, strengthened my faith, helped me overcome trials, and He touched the lives of others through my service. I'll never fully grasp all that God accomplished through me during my time in Iraq. That is, until I stand before Him in Heaven. But for now, I have the peace of knowing that—despite age, doubts, fears, and any limitations—I was obedient to Him. Even today, I'm experiencing the joy of fulfilling God's purpose for my life.

And that's the point of this book.

Baghdad and Beyond

My story begins in Iraq. I'll share with you the sights, sounds, aromas, and emotions that are a part of daily survival in a war zone. But along the way, I'll take you back to my youth, and I'll walk you through some of the milestones of my life. I'll reveal the faith lessons I've learned, as well as my secrets to a meaningful journey with God.

But before we get started, understand this: By no means is Grambo some kind of Bible-wielding, spiritually muscle-bound *super-saint*! I'm just striving to be a faithful servant. And I take seriously these important words Jesus spoke nearly two-thousand years ago:

> "Love the Lord your God with all your heart and with all your soul and with all your mind.' This is the first and greatest commandment. And the second is like it: 'Love your neighbor as yourself.' All the Law and the Prophets hang on these two commandments" (Matthew 22:37-40).

This Scripture sums up how I strive to live—and what I desire others to experience as they get to know me and "walk in my boots!" My prayer is that you'll be encouraged by my testimony. Whether you're a new mom or a grandmother like me, whether you're single, married, or widowed—I hope you'll encounter God on these pages . . . and choose to embrace an abundant life. It's my greatest desire that you'll muster up the courage to plunge deep into the adventure of knowing intimately and serving passionately our Lord and Savior—a Man named Jesus Christ.

What to Expect From this Book

So, exactly what kind of a book is this? The memoirs of a Christian adventurer? A 40-day devotional journey? Stories of faith for Christian women? A battle cry for future Grambos? In many ways, it's all of the above.

So grab a cup of tea and snuggle up with these pages. Share this book with the ladies at church or in the workplace. Study this resource with your family. Each chapter is short and is anchored on a Scriptural truth. And tucked within my stories is practical wisdom that I've applied to my life; biblical insights that I'm sure will relate to your circumstances, too—perhaps even the *men* in your life!

As we start this journey together, consider these words of wisdom from the past. They were written by an amazing woman of faith, Joy Davidman. (She was the wife of Christian scholar C.S. Lewis.)

> "Our generation has never seen a man crucified except in sugary religious art. . . . A crucified slave beside the Roman road screamed until his voice died and then hung, a filthy, festering clot of flies, sometimes for days—a living man whose hands and feet were swollen masses of gangrenous meat. That is what our Lord took upon Himself, 'that through death he might destroy him that had the power of death, that is, the devil; and deliver them, who through fear of death were all their lifetime subject to bondage.' 'Thou shalt not' is the beginning of wisdom. But

the end of wisdom, the new law, is 'Thou shalt.' To be Christian is to be old? Not a bit of it. To be Christian is to be reborn, and free, and unafraid, and immortally young."

Smoke on the Mountain, © *1954, Westminster Press, p. 20.*

1

PEACE IN A BUNKER

Assurance

He who dwells in the shelter of the Most High will rest in the shadow of the Almighty. I will say of the Lord, "He is my refuge and my fortress, my God, in whom I trust." Surely he will save you from the fowler's snare and from the deadly pestilence. He will cover you with his feathers, and under his wings you will find refuge, his faithfulness will be your shield and rampart.
Psalm 91:1-4

KABOOM . . . BOOM!

My room lit up with a bright flash and the walls rattled violently. I rolled onto the floor and squinted toward a window. Frantic voices filled the walkways outside as soldiers and civilians ran for the bunkers.

Has a rocket hit our building?

With my heart pounding—and thankful to be alive—I scrambled in the darkness to find my helmet and vest. It was my second night in Baghdad, and regardless of my intense training, I quickly realized that there is no way to fully prepare for the frightening realities of war. Experiencing a barrage of gunfire and explosions is a lot like being hooked up to a set of jumper cables.

Instant adrenaline!

I called out to a girl in the next bedroom. She had only been in country for a week prior to me, so I assumed—and rightly so—that she would

1

probably be even more terrified than me. After all, I had about forty years on her.

"Evelyn, I'm OK," she yelled back. "Have we been hit?"

"Don't know," I said, "but let's get out of here. The bunker. Head to the bunker—NOW!"

My suite-mate and I decided to forego our robes and evacuate in pajamas, flak-jackets, and helmets. I imagine the two of us were quite a sight.

The equipment was heavy, even for a young person, so I helped her pull on her vest. Then we opened the front door and rushed into the night.

Camp Victory was dry and hot, and a mixture of smoke and diesel filled the air. More lights flashed in the distance, and the ground shook again—followed by more screams and frantic chatter. My legs and arms were moving faster than I ever thought was possible, especially for a grandmother! And just ahead, I spotted my goal: the entrance to a bunker. Would I make it?

Faster, Evelyn, I told myself. *Run faster.*

As amazing as it sounds in a moment like this, I felt God's peace take hold. Somehow I knew everything would be OK.

By the time we were inside, I was calm and unafraid.

The bunkers were just metal shipping containers with sandbags piled on top and around the sides. We huddled in the closest one with about a dozen others. More stragglers came in as we waited for the all clear to return to our beds.

The more experienced among us explained the missiles were outgoing, not incoming, so we covered our ears and prayed for the safety of our soldiers and ourselves.

The inside of the shelter was, like almost everything else in the camp, covered with sand. It was stuffy and cramped and uncomfortable, but I was thankful to be safe and with others who had experienced this before.

While it was pitch black, I was quite aware of those around me. Some people stood, some sat. Some talked, and some remained quiet. Some were prayerful, some were boisterous. The range of reaction was striking, but the singular common behavior I observed, then and thereafter in these situations, was respectfulness. Everyone was solicitous of those around them, regardless of their tenure.

I suppose the *long-termers* remembered how they had felt their first time, and the *newbies* were grateful to be around others who had previously been through it. But everyone acted decently toward the others. It was wonderful to experience such disparate individuals come together in crisis and support each other so completely.

As I sat quietly, my mind drifted back to a dream just before the explosion had jolted me awake. . . .

I was eighteen again, watching from a distance as Bobby Dykes told Shirley Harris he had fallen in love with me. At least that's what I discovered later. They were engaged, and Bobby had driven two days without sleep when he'd suddenly realized he was about to marry the wrong woman. He bravely told her before I knew anything at all about it.

We were friends, but I had no idea he had such strong feelings for me at the time. Regardless, Bobby was not the type to hedge his bets, seeking to test my emotions before breaking it off with Shirley. Even at twenty-one, he was honest and respectful in all things, and whatever my feelings, he could not marry her if he loved another.

Oh how I missed Bobby—especially now. I missed his strong brown eyes and gentle spirit. He was confident, reassuring, and very much a man on a mission.

In all our years together, he never took the easy road . . . and neither did I.

Suddenly, my focus returned to the bunker.

A woman beside me, who was also new to Iraq, began to sob and shake hysterically. I could not see her in the dark but I felt her anguish.

"I don't want to be here!" she cried. "I didn't know it would be like this!"

I reached for her hand and she gripped it tightly. As the sound of rockets above us continued, I prayed aloud: "Oh, Father in Heaven . . . please be with my friend here. Ease her fears. Help her to be still and know that You are God."

She rocked and prayed with me, gradually calming.

Others in the bunker that night later told me how much they appreciated my efforts to comfort that poor, frightened woman. I never met her in the light of day, and no one ever admitted to her identity, but I was grateful to be there next to her that night.

I believe God placed me there for her, at that time. I've always received great satisfaction from helping others. It's my greatest desire to be wherever the Lord can use me in such ways.

After I married Bobby, we spent several years overseas as missionaries before he accepted his last pastorate in the United States. Those were some of the happiest years of my life. We shared not only a love of service, but an adventurous spirit.

It was clear to me that night in the bunker, that Baghdad was a place where I could make good use of both.

This was the first of many hours I would spend in bunkers over the next three years, and always in the midst of these attacks, the Lord would give me peace. This was not true for everyone. After each attack, while many lay awake, I would go back to my room and thank God for His protection, and fall fast asleep.

The next day when I awoke, I was eager to serve the Lord once more. I knew I was in the right place. I knew God had much more to accomplish through me.

Many years ago, during a particularly traumatic experience, God had blessed me with the assurance He was not finished with me yet.

2
GOD'S DIVINE PLAN

Purpose

And we know that in all things God works for the good of those who love him, who have been called according to His purpose
Romans 8:28

Regardless of the challenges I encounter or the personal sacrifices I'm required to make, I desire to be exactly where God calls me so I can fulfill His *purpose* for my life. That's why I served in Iraq. But it was a single life-changing event years earlier that gave me the courage to always say *"YES!"* when God says *"GO!"*

Let me take you back to that pivotal moment in my life. . . .

It was the summer of 1986, a cool, starry night in rural Indiana. My husband was preaching at a church just outside the annual Lands Flea Market near Hagerstown. I had just left an evening service and was driving back to the campground where we were staying for the duration of the market.

Little did I realize, teenagers had apparently knocked down a sign that warned of a dangerous turn. I guess it was some kind of morbid prank. The straight road abruptly ended and veered sharply to the right. I was traveling about forty miles per hour and came upon it so quickly I knew the car would flip if I tried to negotiate the turn.

Just ahead was a cornfield, which seemed like a better option than rolling the car, so I hit the brake and kept the wheel straight, unaware of a gravel berm at a dead end.

When I hit the barrier, I launched my poor son's Dodge Charger into the air, smashing my head against the windshield.

What happened next may sound unbelievable, but I assure you it's true.

At the moment of impact I felt my spirit leave my body. It was as if my very being, my consciousness, simply floated away from my physical self.

All the fear and pain and adrenaline one experiences during an event such as this simply switched off, leaving me to watch the results of the crash from above without apprehension. It was not so much a detached feeling as it was peaceful.

I had the sensation of great height, yet as I looked down I could easily see the expression on my face, the tight grip of my hands on the steering wheel, and every detail of the entire scene as clearly as if I were watching it unfold on a television set from a few feet away.

I watched myself as the car landed nose-down in a small, hidden ravine separating the cornfield from the road. I remember realizing the split-second choice I made to avoid the turn was the correct one. Had the car flipped, I would have landed upside down in the ravine and possibly drowned in the water where the Charger came to rest.

As I observed myself in the car, I began to hear voices. One, I heard clearly on my left, the other came from my right. The voice on my left exultantly exclaimed "I told you I'd get her today!"

But on my right, the other voice said, "No. Not today." It was steady and measured, and its calmness reinforced my own. "Not today."

I realized later the accident occurred six years to the hour after the death of my first husband, and father of my children, Bobby Dykes.

I have come to believe the voices were spirits representing good and evil, fighting to claim me for their own. I don't know how long they argued, but I remember distinctly the voice on my right saying firmly, "I'm not finished with her yet." And suddenly I was back in the car, awake and in terrible pain.

But I was alive. God wasn't finished with me yet.

I realized immediately I needed to get away from where I'd landed. Not only was I badly injured, but if another car came by they would likely crash into the ravine, too.

I tried to open my door but it wouldn't budge, so I reached across to the passenger door. It, too, was immovable.

I looked up at the starry sky and the beautiful quarter moon, and spoke aloud to the Lord.

"God, I don't understand," I said. "I don't know what just happened, except that you've allowed me to stay here on earth. Why, I don't know. But there must be a reason. I trust you, Lord. I trust you to help me get out of this car so I can fulfill whatever purpose you have for me."

When I reached for the car door again it opened easily.

The following day when a tow truck driver came for the car, I was told he took one look and decided there was no possible way I had been able to open that door. The car was just too badly damaged. He was certain someone very strong had pulled it open for me.

I cannot disagree.

Once the door was open I realized how badly I had been injured. I was in great pain and blood flowed freely down my face.

When I finally managed to swing my legs out onto the ground, I collapsed. I couldn't walk, let alone stand.

Once again, I asked for God's strength, and He answered. I slowly pulled myself up the side of the ravine, grabbing handfuls of grass and whatever else I could find to slowly inch my way back up to the road.

It was extremely difficult, but as the Bible says in Philippians 4:13, "I can do all things through Christ, who strengthens me."

I made it to the top.

Now I needed to get away from the dead end. Any other car that came by would end up as I had, so I half crawled, half scooted up the road. I could hear the distant sounds of the flea market across the still, crisp night, but had no way of signaling anyone there.

When I was far enough away from the end of the road to feel relatively safe, I sat and rested, praying someone would happen by. It was a seldom traveled road, especially at night, but I was not afraid because I truly felt the Lord had not brought me this far to allow me to die.

After about an hour, I saw the lights of a truck turning onto the road from the direction of the flea market. Though feeling quite weak by this time, I gathered all my strength to sit up and wave my arms in an attempt to attract the attention of whoever was approaching.

Two young men were in the vehicle, one of whom had just bought the truck the day before and was taking his cousin out for a ride. I can only imagine the shock they felt when their headlights revealed a bloody woman sitting on the side of this deserted gravel road in her Sunday clothes, frantically waving her arms in the air. I found out later the driver almost never took this particular route, but was feeling adventurous with his new purchase and decided to explore a bit.

I have always been blessed with adventurous souls.

When I told these two young men I'd been involved in a car accident, they grew wary. My car was not visible from the road, and I believe they thought I could be part of a prank or, worse, some sort of trick to rob them.

But I directed the driver to the ravine, and when he found the car they realized my story was truthful and helped me into their truck.

It reminded me of the Good Samaritan, who helped the waylaid traveler he found bleeding by the side of the road. It was truly a blessing these two young Samaritans also didn't hesitate to help in my time of need.

They drove me to the flea market where my husband rushed me to the hospital in Richmond, which was quicker than calling an ambulance.

I was covered with horrible bruises all over my body. My chest hit the steering wheel so hard it actually bent the wheel, and my knees collapsed the lower console. I also suffered serious head trauma, but thankfully sustained no permanent damage. Almost everything healed over time.

Almost.

The single lasting physical injury I carry with me to this day is one that also serves to deepen my faith, even as I endure its painful effects.

The bones in my right heel were crushed. A specialist in Indianapolis, who treated many similar injuries sustained by race car drivers, told me then it was better to abstain from surgery, because I would never be able to bend my foot at the ankle if it was repaired at that time. He advised I would do fine until my sixties, when it would likely become quite painful. Ironically, nearly twenty years later, in my sixties, I felt moved to go to Iraq.

After my accident, I knew without question God had a purpose for my life. There is a reason I'm here. Whether, as I thought at the time, it was to see my children and grandchildren grown, or something else entirely, I didn't know.

But there's a reason.

Perhaps it was to go to Iraq to provide aid and comfort to our soldiers. Perhaps it's all these things—with more to come.

Whatever the reason, I'm still here. And I'm ready to fulfill that purpose, regardless of what it is or where it takes me.

Romans 8:28 says, "And we know that in all things God works for the good of those who love him, who have been called according to His purpose." I believe my car accident was supposed to happen just as it did as a way for God to remind me that there is a purpose for my life. And I carry the lesson of that night with me.

Every day since my accident, when I wake up and put my feet on the floor, I feel the pain of that distant injury and I thank God I'm alive.

And then I ask Him, "What is my purpose today?"

And I do my very best to fulfill it.

3

SUITING UP FOR BATTLE

Preparation

Finally, be strong in the Lord and in his mighty power. Put on the full armor of God so that you can take your stand against the devil's schemes. For our struggle is not against flesh and blood, but against the rulers, against the authorities, against the powers of this dark world and against the spiritual forces of evil in the heavenly realms.
Ephesians 6:10-12

"Gas, gas, gas!" the instructor yelled.

I fumbled with the bulky mask that completed my oh-so-stylish chemical deterrent suit, finally getting it over my head before the unpleasant odor wafted through the room.

I glanced quickly at the others and saw with somewhat absurd satisfaction I was not the last person to "get my lid on."

I quickly remembered to check the hem of my suit to ensure the masking tape formed a tight seal against the top of my oversized boots and thought to myself, *Evelyn, what on earth have you gotten yourself into?*

It was October 2004, and I was standing with a group of several dozen future civilian contractors in a vacant J.C. Penney store in suburban Houston, decked out in full chemical protective gear, preparing, in my seventh decade, to go to Iraq.

The drills the instructors led were beginning to cause me concern. This was serious business, and while I did not doubt my decision to sign up, I was definitely wondering just exactly what the future held.

A few weeks before, the agency I managed in northeast Louisiana announced they would soon be closing offices all over the state. I supervised staff that coordinated long term care for Medicaid recipients. I took great joy in helping families with elderly parents. My own father was in his eighties at the time, so I understood quite well the burdens and blessings long term care represented.

Before that I counseled and provided aid to teenage mothers, which was also spiritually rewarding. I remembered my days as a young mother, and my heart went out to those who lacked family and friends to help them at such a formative time in a woman's life. I was blessed to be raised in a loving home, and I always strove to provide the same for my children.

But now I had to make a career change.

To look at me one might never think I would consider adding contractor in Iraq to my resume, but I have always had an adventurous spirit.

It never failed to evoke surprise, even among friends who knew me well, the story of a month-long camping trip I took with my husband Bobby and two other young soldiers back in 1963. It was six-thousand miles each way in a Volkswagen Bug from France to Jerusalem and back again. I was twenty-one years-old.

Now at age sixty-three, here I was, planning to travel seven thousand miles into a war zone. The Lord truly works in mysterious ways.

I drew comfort from my life experiences, and the many unplanned detours that profoundly affected my life in unexpected ways. I believed then, as I do now, that the challenges we face only serve to make us stronger if we give our life to the Lord and trust Him to provide the strength we need to make it through each trial.

I have often wondered, as many do, why God allows us to be burdened at times with more than we feel we can bear. I've discovered that it's often because He wants us to come to Him with our problems. He yearns to strengthen our faith and grant us the ability to persevere. It's a wondrous circle of faith.

In the past, I had experienced the peace of knowing I was in the perfect will of God, and I was determined to attain that same feeling before I made the final decision to go to Iraq.

There were so many negative reports in the news about the war, with kidnappings and beheadings—it was not a place I really wanted to be.

But after discussing the risks and hardships I would certainly face, and after much prayer and consideration, I found the inner peace that came with the knowledge this was the direction God wanted my life to take.

Several months earlier, my former administrative assistant and dear friend Sharon Gillis had left for Iraq, which also helped reassure me that I was capable of doing this. We are close in age, and I felt better knowing she was there when I made my decision.

I called my sons and their families together to break the news that, God willing, their mother and grandmother would be going to Iraq. They were surprised but supportive, and after much discussion and many questions, we rejoiced and prayed together.

There were preliminary evaluations to pass, so I immediately began making plans. I've always been the type of person who, once she decides to do something, enjoys tackling a task head on. I thrive on hard work, especially when I know myself to be on God's path.

Much to my surprise, my younger son Byron arrived two days later to tell me that he, too, would be applying for a position in Iraq. After talking it over with his wife, Stephanie, he'd decided he simply didn't want me going alone.

I was proud, appreciative, and fearful all at the same time, and accepted his decision with a full heart. That night I prayed for us both, and fell asleep with the knowledge God would watch over each of us just as my sweet son planned to watch over me.

Byron's son Bryton, who was four at the time, and my older son Bren's boys, Seth, age nine, and Gevin, age six, were all very excited about their grandmother going off to war.

Except they didn't call me grandmother. They each had strong, individual personalities, and had come up with their own separate names for me.

To Seth, the eldest, I was Grams. To Gevin, Grammy, and to the youngest, Bryton, I was Mimi. But this was soon to change.

I don't know if it was the prospect of only long term, long distance communication which spurred it, or the fact they understood, despite their ages, just how serious a sojourn this would be, but these young boys put their heads together and decided, with military precision and effectiveness, that they must do their duty as my grandsons and unify my grandmotherly identity.

After much discussion (and I suspect a little help from my son), I was heretofore to be referred to, by them all, as *Grambo.*

I made it through two weeks of processing, including the special training women received regarding personal protection and slightly different travel requirements, and left on October 28, 2004, for Frankfurt, Dubai, and Baghdad.

I felt excited, scared, and confused all at the same time.

But like the nicknames assigned by my grandchildren, soon my emotions came together and I felt completely at peace, knowing I was once again right where God wanted me to be.

Grambo was about to invade Baghdad.

4
My Mentor, My Mother

Foundations

²You yourselves are our letter, written on our hearts, known and read by everybody. ³You show that you are a letter from Christ, the result of our ministry, written not with ink but with the Spirit of the living God, not on tablets of stone but on tablets of human hearts
² Corinthians 3: 2-3

I never heard my mother raise her voice. She was a gentle woman who personified dignity and grace, and from an early age, I learned by example to treat others with the same patience and kindness she showed everyone she met.

Hope Webb overcame many hardships during her life without complaint, and instilled in me the belief there was nothing I could not do if I worked hard and trusted the Lord to guide me. She encouraged me not to feel limited because I was female, which wasn't a universally accepted concept in those days.

She was a devoutly religious woman, dedicated to her family, always putting others before herself. She loved laughter and music and prayer, and those things were never in short supply in the home she made for us.

My brother Jerry and I both took piano lessons from an early age, but the instrument came much easier to him. As a result, many times I would get frustrated and cry at the piano when I felt I couldn't 'get' a particular piece.

Mother would kneel right down on the floor next to where I sat on the bench, take my hand, and pray that I would receive peace of mind and find the joy in my lessons. This never failed to calm my nerves and is a foundation of my belief in the healing power of prayer.

Many times in Iraq, before the soldiers went out on missions, I would take their hands and pray with them, calming their fears much as my mother did mine.

What a wonderful feeling to know that wherever we are, from a piano bench in Louisiana to a military camp in the middle of a war zone, comfort is always available if we simply stop and speak to our Heavenly Father.

Often on Saturdays, Mother and I would take the bus to Greenwood Road and catch the trolley to downtown Shreveport.

We'd get off at Texas Street, in the heart of the shopping district, and walk down one side of the street and back up the other, enjoying the day and looking for any new clothes displayed in the windows since our last visit.

When I found a dress I liked, my mother would examine it carefully, turning it inside and out, committing each stitch and seam to memory.

Upon our return at the end of the day, she would trace the design on newspaper and cut out a pattern from which she would later create a perfect copy of the dress for me to wear to school or church. I was always in fashion at a fraction of the cost of store-bought clothes, and the envy of my girlfriends. No one would ever guess my entire wardrobe was handmade unless I told them so.

As I got older, it gradually became more difficult for her to make my clothes. By my sophomore year in high school she simply wasn't strong enough to continue the practice, which I know deeply saddened her.

Mother suffered from emphysema though she never smoked, as well as multiple sclerosis. Unfortunately, the latter disease was misdiagnosed when she was a teenager, leaving one of her eyes permanently damaged.

At the age of seventeen she collapsed and was thought by doctors to have suffered a stroke . Surgery was performed on her eye in a failed attempt to correct the resulting impaired vision. Years later, it was discovered she was actually exhibiting early symptoms of MS, and had the surgery not been performed, it is very likely her eye would have returned to normal over time. Instead, the eye remained misaligned the rest of her life.

Still, she never complained, and even enjoyed reading to me for hours on end when I was a child, instilling in me a love of literature I carry to this day. I remember she often told me she hoped I would one day read to her the same way, should it ever become too difficult for her to continue.

In spite of her ailments, she was very active during my early childhood. She often wrestled across the floor with Jerry and me, tickling us until we cried from laughter. Years later, when she was too weak to comb her hair without help, the bittersweet memories of those times we shared were treasured by us all.

Still, ours was a happy and busy home. On the weekends there always seemed to be school friends over to play badminton or volleyball, and Jerry's friends would run in and out on their way to nearby fields for ball games.

Mother was always eager to talk and laugh with the children, offering a cold drink and asking after their parents. She relished watching us do the things she could no longer do, and loved to see happiness in others.

During the week, whenever Jerry and I came home from school, Mother was waiting with refreshments at the kitchen table and anxious to hear all about our day. We would talk and laugh until she had to start supper. Jerry was two years my junior, but being a boy he eventually wanted to grab a snack and run outside with his friends, so later on it became just Mother and me. We grew even closer as a result of these times together.

One such day stands out in my mind very clearly. I came home a bit earlier than usual, walked into the house, and everything was very quiet. Most days when I arrived home after school I would hear my mother bustling about in the kitchen or another room in the house. But this day there was only silence. I was about to call out for my mother when I heard a voice from her bedroom.

I walked toward the door, and as I got closer I realized she was praying. I had heard her pray before, of course, but the sound of her speaking aloud to the Lord while all alone in her bedroom moved me deeply.

I really felt God's presence at that moment, and quietly went back out to the porch to respect her time of fellowship. Matthew 6:5-6 says, "And when you pray, you must not be like the hypocrites. For they love to stand and pray in the synagogues and at the street corners, that they may be seen by others. Truly, I say to you, they have received their reward. But when you pray, go into your room and shut the door and pray to your Father who is in secret. And your Father who sees in secret will reward you."

I waited outside until my normal time of arrival from school, and had my usual visit with Mother about the day's activities, but I always remembered how she embodied the spirit of those verses. Her love for the Lord was never just for show, but a very real and personal relationship.

Of course she loved to go to church, especially on Wednesday nights, but as she grew weaker it became more and more difficult for her. During the last three or four years of her life she would actually begin preparing for the evening service on Wednesday morning, so long did it take her to get ready in her weakened state.

During this time I was in my late twenties, and though Bobby and I had traveled quite a bit early in our marriage for his ministry, I was very grateful to be in Shreveport during my mother's final years. She had become such an inspiration to me. As I grew older I realized how much she had struggled to overcome obstacles, and her words from years before took on even more resonance. "You can do anything you put your mind to, Evelyn, as long as you work hard and trust in the Lord."

When I was in Iraq, many of the young soldiers told me I reminded them of their mothers at home, and found my presence comforting. I always was very conscious to speak to them in a calm and reassuring manner, much like the way my mother spoke to me.

This is not to say she wasn't firm when she needed to be. A single stern look from my mother in church ended all thoughts of misbehavior in an instant. I often imagined she knew what I was thinking before I did. Jerry and I were typical children, but we became quite well behaved, especially in God's house. Our younger brother Verdell came along much later, and he too was a well behaved child.

When I became an adult, my mother still served as a reminder of good Christian behavior. When my firstborn was about a year old, I took him along with my mother to a department store to pick up a promised order. As I held my squirming son I was eager to finish my shopping and leave, but was told the merchandise was unavailable. Unhappy with the service, I lost my temper and spoke rather sharply to the clerk.

When we got back to the car, my mother told me how disappointed she was in my behavior. "Evelyn," she said, "you represent Christ in all things. To everyone you meet, you are his representative. When you talk to someone like that, you're falling short of His expectations for you as a Christian. Always think before you speak."

Here I was, a mother myself, still learning simple kindnesses from her. To this day I think back to that conversation whenever I am tempted to speak in anger to another human being. Long after her passing she's still minding my manners!

In my many conversations with the young soldiers in Iraq, I felt her calm spirit and Christian example influencing my behavior and helping me to comfort them in my own small way.

And I knew Mother was smiling down on me.

5

GRAMBO INVADES BAGHDAD

Faith

And without faith it is impossible to please God, because anyone who comes to him must believe that he exists and that he rewards those who earnestly seek him.
Hebrews 11:6

In October of 2004 I arrived in Baghdad ready for anything but still surprised at what I found. It's another instance where you really cannot adequately prepare; you just have to jump in with both feet and trust the Lord to guide you.

Often in life we must take a 'leap of faith,' and my initial experience in Iraq was definitely one of those times.

As I said, sand was pretty much everywhere, which of course I expected in the middle of the desert.

But what I failed to consider and what no one adequately explained beforehand is the effect when it rains. There was mud absolutely everywhere. I've never seen so much mud in all my life, and there was simply no way you could avoid it.

It rained for several days shortly after I arrived, and not having appropriate footwear, I had to wear my chemical boots, which were very large as they were designed to fit over army boots.

The mud made everything very slick, so it was like crossing an ice rink wearing roller skates that were three sizes too big. Just wrong every which way you look at it. Several times that first day I nearly slipped head over heels, and wearing a long skirt and those enormous boots I guess I was a sight to behold. I know I managed to tickle quite a few soldiers when they got a look at my big shoes splashing around the camp.

Talk about jumping in with both feet!

Still, I thanked the Lord I was where He wanted me to be, and trusted Him to protect and guide me. Truly, this was a leap of faith.

My first days in Camp Victory were physically difficult. I had packed several large bottles of over-the-counter medication from the states to ease the pain in my foot from that long ago accident, but they disappeared from my bags as they went through customs in Dubai.

And on top of my footwear problem, I also had to wear a heavy flak jacket and helmet for days at a time because of increased mortar attacks and other such insurgent activities. Sometimes, carrying around that extra sixty pounds really tired me out, let me tell you.

However, I was very blessed in other ways, such as meeting up with my dear friend Sharon when I first arrived.

It was wonderful to see her again. She had been in Iraq for almost a year and was an old pro by the time I saw her smiling face waiting in front of the processing center at Camp Victory.

She was able to take me around the camp, which is located on airport grounds about three miles from Baghdad International Airport, just west of the city.

Palaces and other buildings scattered across the camp were being used by the military, most for offices, some for sleeping quarters. I was eventually assigned a room in a modular building in the middle of what had once been Saddam's private wheat field.

Walls completely surrounded the entire area, which also included a beautiful hunting lodge and fields where game had been kept. There had even been an alligator pit next to the lodge at one time which was purportedly used for nefarious purposes by Saddam and his sons. The pit was filled in and eventually became a parking lot for the lodge which had been converted to an MWR site.

It's wonderful that a place formerly used for evil deeds now provides morale, welfare, and recreational support to the very men and women whose actions ended such terrible abuses.

The palaces were quite opulent, and I was reminded of King Nebuchadnezzar from the book of Daniel, who prided himself on his monuments and buildings, but was humbled by God and cast into the wilderness until he learned to honor the Lord above himself.

Saddam reportedly named a division of his Republican Guard after Nebuchadnezzar. It's too bad he didn't learn the same lesson.

I felt real sadness for the Iraqi people, who lived among such beauty and natural resources squandered by a tyrannical dictator.

Driving around the camp, I was struck by how lovely the area must have been before the war. There were many canals lined by bulrushes along the water, which reminded me of how Moses was placed in a basket made of such reeds in the river Nile to spare him from the wrath of Pharaoh.

Everywhere I looked I saw evidence of God's grace. Even in a war zone surrounded by many who would do harm, I was joyful in the presence of the Lord, and again thanked him for leading me here. I asked for His continued strength to endure whatever trials He set before me, and my prayers were answered daily.

On top of all the rain and mud there was a lot of increased activity around camp during this time because the military was preparing for the second invasion of Fallujah.

Fallujah is a city in the Al Anbar province of Iraq about forty miles west of Baghdad. It's known in Iraq as the city of mosques because there are so many within its borders and the surrounding area.

Fallujah was mostly spared during the initial invasion in 2003 but was devastated by the looting which took place afterwards. It was mostly populated by Sunnis and had been a stronghold of Saddam within the area known as the Sunni Triangle.

Several months before, four military contractors had been killed there by insurgents and their bodies were paraded as trophies, which became a major news story all over the world. Shortly thereafter the Coalition forces went in to capture the city but fought the insurgents to a draw.

I had arrived just before the start of the ultimately successful second attempt to take control of Fallujah, Operation Phantom Fury.

It always tore at my heart to see the soldiers who were on their way to missions in Fallujah. I prayed constantly for their safe return.

Though I heard nightly the planes overhead and the distant explosions, I was not afraid. Though I felt the daily mortars that landed in or near the camp, I did not despair.

But on only my second day at work when I received the news a medic with a wife and three children had been killed at a nearby prison site, I was moved to tears for the first of many times during my stay in Iraq.

I did not know the man, I only heard of his death through a co-worker. But the thought of this civilian doctor who left his family to travel halfway across the world to tend the needs of others truly touched my heart. It was a stark reminder to me the problems of boots and clothes and pain pills really didn't amount to much in the grand scheme of things.

Perspective is everything, and as I said a prayer for the man's family before bed that night, I also asked the Lord to always make me aware of the important things in life.

I don't think the American public always understands how much support the armed forces require, and the increasingly large role which civilian contractors must play in modern warfare.

It's terribly sad when wars must be fought, but when our brave men and women are in harm's way it's comforting to know there are those like that dedicated young doctor willing to risk his life to provide care for those who provide such support.

I am humbled the Lord chose me to assist in this task, and hark back to the lesson of Shadrach, Meshach, and Abednego, also from the Book of Daniel.

Nebuchadnezzar threw them into a fiery furnace for refusing to worship false idols, but the Lord sent an angel to protect them, and they emerged unharmed.

Those three young men knew what was important in life.

I resolved to remain steadfast and unafraid, and trust in the protection of the Lord, so that I, too, would come through the fire unscathed.

6

LIFE'S SURPRISE-FILLED JOURNEYS

God's Ways

⁸ "For my thoughts are not your thoughts, neither are your ways my ways," declares the LORD.⁹ "As the heavens are higher than the earth, so are my ways higher than your ways and my thoughts than your thoughts.
Isaiah 55:8-9

One evening when I was fifteen, my father suddenly looked across the dinner table at me, and said, "Evelyn, I need you to promise me something."

Without a moment's hesitation, I replied, "Of course," never anticipating for an instant his next words.

"Until you're married, don't cross my threshold pregnant."

My mother dropped her fork, my brother Jerry dropped his jaw, and I wanted to drop off the face of the earth from embarrassment.

"Dad-dy."

"I mean it, Evelyn."

My mother looked over at my youngest brother Verdell, who was only two at the time, but he was happily playing with his food as children his age are wont to do.

Jerry found his voice and giggled, but a quick look from my father quieted him immediately, as looks from my father were wont to do.

Daddy was a large, outgoing man with a wonderful sense of humor but I knew he was not joking about this. As the disciplinarian in the family, when he laid down the law, there was no argument to be made.

I looked to my mother, but her face was unreadable as she waited patiently for my father to explain his concern. I had never once heard the two of them argue, and I knew whatever Daddy was thinking she was assuredly on the same page.

"I know all about hormones at your age. But there are some things I will not tolerate. Do you understand?"

I thought I saw the hint of a smile on my mother's face when Daddy mentioned hormones, but his serious tone drew my focus back to his serious eyes.

"I want to go to college," I told him, hoping he would drop the subject. It just was not something I wanted to discuss with him at that moment.

My parents exchanged a look, and finally my father said, "Promise me."

"Daddy, I promise," I said quickly, hoping this little inquisition would soon be over.

Our family suppers were usually so enjoyable!

My answer seemed to satisfy him, and he reached across the table and gave my hand a squeeze, never dropping his eyes from my own.

I could tell he was trying to reassure me of his trust, so I smiled and went back to my supper, ignoring Jerry, whose exaggerated lack of interest I could plainly see out of the corner of one eye. My father noticed it too, apparently.

"So Jerry," my father said, "how are you doing in social studies?"

Jerry's jaw dropped once more and as he stammered an answer my father gave me a sly wink. My father was tough, but fair.

Daddy had known Bobby's father, George, but because the Dykes family moved to California when Bobby was quite young, he and I never actually met until his family moved back to Louisiana when I was fourteen years old.

Bobby was outgoing and gregarious, but being three years older he didn't show much interest in me back then. I had a little bit of a schoolgirl crush for a short time after he returned, but that was to be expected at my age and faded quickly. I had no idea, of course, that this friend of the family who'd recently arrived from California so tan and handsome would be my husband only four years later.

25

We had only sporadic contact until my senior year in high school. Bobby was attending Centenary College in Shreveport and working for his father. He often made road trips to California to purchase vehicles at auction for resale on his father's car lot.

As for me, I was also planning to attend Centenary in the fall on a scholarship. I spent half the day in my high school classes and the other half at Ayers Business School. My father insisted I take a secretarial/business course because, as he put it, I would "be okay no matter what happened." I had no idea at the time how prescient his advice was.

I had also been accepted to play the oboe with the Shreveport Metropolitan Symphony, so I was especially excited about the year to come.

I felt like my life was just beginning, and my future was laid out before me like a shining pathway.

I soon found out the Lord had other plans.

My mother related the following story to me upon hearing it from Bobby's mother after a very interesting few months in my young life:

During a trip home from California in May of 1959, Bobby was having a tough time choosing a gift for his fiancée. He and his mother Doris were driving home with a car they'd purchased, and had crossed the border at El Paso to check the little shops in Juarez for a colorful skirt for Shirley Harris. They were to be married in August, and Bobby thought she'd like something festive to wear during what was sure to be a typically scorching Louisiana summer.

But every time he found something, he couldn't help but think it would look perfect on me. His mother smiled but remained silent, following Bobby from store to store, each time picking out a skirt which he just knew would look great on his good friend Evelyn.

Finally, he found a somewhat garish but colorful skirt covered with sequins, and held it up for his mother to see. She saw a look of realization cross his face, and suddenly he blurted out, "Mother I'm going to give this to Evelyn!"

Doris just smiled. She had secretly been hoping for this, as had her husband. Unbeknownst to Bobby, George Dykes had been calling while his wife and son were in California to see if I was interested in Bobby.

I had not considered this, and was actually dating another boy around this time, anyway. I figured Mr. Dykes' curiosity was due to pre-wedding jitters or the fact he and my father had been friends for such a long time. Bobby and I had never expressed romantic feelings for each other, and since he was to be married soon it was the furthest thing from my mind.

As I've already related, as soon as Bobby realized his true feelings he drove straight back to Louisiana from Mexico to break the news to Shirley.

She and I were attending a huge Church Youth Camp in Alexandria at the time. I saw Bobby enter the tabernacle, find Shirley, and though I didn't know what they were saying at the time, I believe I understood in my heart.

Three months later, Bobby and I were married.

Many things changed in my life as a result.

I never used my scholarship and never played a single note with the symphony in Shreveport.

My father's advice was correct on all counts, from hormones to business college, the latter of which has served me well my entire life, continuing through my time in Iraq.

My mother, who had been praying for the same thing as Bobby's mother, was cautious but happy, and Daddy gave Bobby permission to marry his only daughter.

I still have that wonderfully garish skirt, with its sequined picture of a Mexican boy dancing with his sweetheart.

It's the most beautiful piece of clothing I own.

We felt like our lives were just beginning, and our future was laid out before us like a shining pathway.

I expected a long and happy life together with my soul-mate, Bobby Dykes.

But once again, the Lord had other plans.

7

NEW LIFE IN A WAR ZONE

Adjustment

⁴Rejoice in the Lord always. I will say it again: Rejoice! ⁵Let your gentleness be evident to all. The Lord is near. ⁶Do not be anxious about anything, but in everything, by prayer and petition, with thanksgiving, present your requests to God. ⁷And the peace of God, which transcends all understanding, will guard your hearts and your minds in Christ Jesus.
Philippians 4:4-7

Aside from the physical exertions of my first week in Baghdad, I was also faced with arduous mental tasks. Namely, learning just what my job would actually entail, how I would best perform my duties, and discovering the answer to that singularly important question all who worked in Iraq asked at one time or another, from the generals to the soldiers to the thousands of civilian support personnel: Would I have the tools I needed to properly do my job?

There were many instances when even the soldiers were lacking necessities such as the best body armor available and proper vehicles, so it should come as no surprise that contractors would also, at times, fall short of optimal resources.

Wars never go exactly as planned, and many times one just has to buckle down and make do. But I am a big believer in preparation and finding the best resources possible to accomplish a particular task. So when I arrived and saw the amount of work which needed to be done, I was daunted but unbowed.

Galatians 6:9 says, "Let us not be weary in well doing, for in due season we shall reap, if we faint not."

I fervently believed in the U.S. mission, and knew the Lord had placed me there to perform my small part in it. I felt secure in the knowledge that He would provide the strength and resources I would need to accomplish my tasks.

I was happy and grateful for the Lord's assignment, and knew perseverance would pay off in the long run.

One of my favorite passages in the Bible begins with the verse Philippians 4:4: "Rejoice in the Lord always. I will say it again: Rejoice!" And I truly did rejoice in the work of the Lord.

On the other hand, it was not easy. Who has not started a new job and gone through that initial period of 'learning the ropes,' and everything that simple phrase can mean? In Iraq, the added pressures of being in a war zone intensified the learning curve quite a bit, to say the least.

I often repeated to myself that verse from Philippians during my first hectic week, and it always brought me comfort, just as it had since I first memorized it in Sunday School as a child.

I knew beforehand the general parameters of the position for which I had been hired, but as I've said, it's one thing to train and prepare for working in Baghdad and another when you actually get your 'boots on the ground.'

I began my 'tour' as a Logistics Supervisor. Logistics encompasses all the calculations necessary to make sure a particular operation or department runs as smoothly as possible. It's the many details which must be tracked to ensure success.

Obviously, the overall logistics of a war effort are enormous, and though I was used to this type of work I fully expected to be faced with what I knew would be enormous challenges.

Logistics includes procurement of equipment and maintenance of same. There are supplies to be obtained, stored, and utilized to their best potential. Not to mention maintaining the storage facilities themselves, and simply keeping track of what has been used, what will be used in the future, and how best to make sure everything actually is available when needed.

We kept track of everything, from how many bags of laundry were washed to the ordering and tracking of vehicles to the number of meals provided and the number of persons using the gyms and computers, and everything was put into reports which were used to promote better efficiency.

Part of my job would be to submit these reports on a daily, weekly, and monthly basis. When I arrived, there was a young Bosnian man named Basim in the office who was working on a computer system to better track all these numbers, but a full year and a half after the initial invasion it was still necessary to compile the figures from each section into the daily and weekly reports, and that task fell to me.

My workday was at least twelve hours, sometimes longer, with no days off. With the Fallujah activities and threats from insurgents during this time, I carried the extra weight of my personal protective equipment, that uncomfortable helmet and vest, even when in the office.

The office itself was a modular building located in a construction area known as Wayne's World. Many who worked and stayed in this area were construction workers, and as those familiar with construction sites and the movie of the same name might surmise, it was generally a little rowdier than the areas where the soldiers stayed.

My direct supervisor, Ed, was a sweet Christian man about my age who had retired from the military a few years prior to coming to Iraq. I enjoyed hearing stories of his wife in Germany and his three grown sons, one of whom was currently serving in the armed forces in Afghanistan. His daughter, Tiffany, was married to a man who was also in the military. We were very compatible and his gentle nature and many kindnesses those first days and weeks were of great help to me as I adjusted to my new environment.

Not all the men were so patient, however, and there was one in particular who made it very clear he didn't think a woman of my age should be where I was, doing what he considered a man's job. I made it clear to him that I was perfectly capable of doing my job as well as he or any man, for that matter.

Ed drove me around that first week to see the various sites where supplies were stored. It would be my responsibility to keep track of these things so that when supplies were requisitioned through our office, I could make sure they were provided. Ed planned to be out in the field once I was trained and able to run the office on my own, so I could see a lot of responsibility would be riding on my shoulders along with that heavy flak jacket.

On my third work day a mortar hit near the DFAC (dining facility) as I ate, and the following morning another one literally shook the office building in which I was working. As I said, it was a modular building, not much more than a large trailer, so when it shook it really shook.

The office was tiny, with seven people working in a space so small everyone would literally have to stand up if anyone needed to leave. Not only that, but the only bathroom available was a port-a-pot! I don't have to tell you I was really looking forward to moving into the permanent facility as soon as it was completed. Wayne's World was not so excellent for this grandmother.

The continuous sound of mortars, helicopters, and other activities served as a constant reminder of the seriousness of our jobs, and my co-workers were mostly supportive and the atmosphere usually congenial. I was struck by the adaptability of human beings with a common purpose.

Shortly after I arrived, the department was dissolved and instead logistics offices were opened to oversee things at each individual camp. This was a bit of a shock, as my position suddenly did not exist in the form I was expecting. It was disconcerting because on top of all the other adjustments I was now filled with uncertainty as to what my job would ultimately involve.

Still, it was a blessing in disguise as that is how I came to be assigned specifically to Morale, Welfare, and Recreation. It was here I believe the Lord sent me to fully realize my potential to serve.

MWR is so much more than stocking supplies and equipment. We are also charged with enhancing the lives of those who defend our nation. We organize leisure activities and entertainment, provide computers so soldiers can communicate with loved ones, and generally attempt to alleviate as much stress as possible from some of the most stressful situations imaginable. We care for those who serve, be they soldiers barely out of their teens or middle-aged national Guardsmen with families and careers back home.

Combat often consists of short periods of intense activity interspersed with periods of waiting. During the down time, a soldier is susceptible to homesickness, depression, and simple boredom, all of which can affect the readiness and cohesiveness the troops need to further their mission.

During World War I, Woodrow Wilson appointee Dr. Raymond Fosdick reported to the Secretary of Defense that..."Morale is as important as ammunition and is just as legitimate a charge against the public treasury."

I took comfort knowing the department to which I had been assigned was in charge of such an important element of the effort in Iraq and the lives of our soldiers.

It was difficult adjusting to my new position at first, but I looked forward to increased opportunities to interact with individual soldiers in need of encouragement and prayer. I was especially grateful for the prayers my friends and family said for me during those first days. Each night, as I reflected on my purpose before going to sleep, it was truly awe-inspiring to realize just how far God had taken me out of my comfort zone in order to do his will. In spite of all the twists and turns my life has taken, He never fails to surprise and inspire me.

All this had been quite an adjustment from what my life was like prior to arriving in Camp Victory, but I found comfort in scripture:

Philippians 4:4-7: "Rejoice in the Lord always. I will say it again: Rejoice!

> Let your gentleness be evident to all. The Lord is near. Do not be anxious about anything, but in everything, by prayer and petition, with thanksgiving, present your requests to God. And the peace of God, which transcends all understanding, will guard your hearts and your minds in Christ Jesus."

8
WAY OF THE RIGHTEOUS

Choices

*⁶ For the LORD watches over the way of the righteous,
but the way of the wicked will perish.
Psalm 1:6*

When Bobby and I got married, it was difficult for us in all the ways typical of young couples. He was twenty-one, and I was eighteen, and while we were both mature for our age, there is always more growing up to do. Neither of our families was especially wealthy, but we were blessed in many other ways.

We both loved the Lord, and desired to devote ourselves to His service. Our parents were close friends, united in fellowship and happy their children had been joined together in the eyes of God.

We both came from loving families who pledged to do whatever they could to help us get started. My father, who was a builder, was able to move us into a house with no down payment.

It was 1959, and we moved into a three bedroom, one bath home for the princely sum of eighty-nine dollars a month. Bobby, who was always very thrifty, was able to purchase furniture with the money he'd saved working for his father at the car lot. I still have the bedroom set from that time!

I went to work for the electric company and Bobby continued his schooling while working for his dad. We were young and very much in love.

I thought we would likely spend many years in our home state of Louisiana, near our families, eventually raising a family of our own.

But later that year Bobby felt called to the ministry. He had always been very outgoing and friendly, able to speak to anyone at any time. He was one of those people who loved talking to others, never hesitating to engage a complete stranger as if they were lifelong friends. Being a girl, I was a little more reticent, but his behavior was infectious and it definitely brought out that side of my personality. Upon reflection, I was amazed I had not seen this potential before, and when he told me of his feelings it felt completely natural as the next chapter of our lives.

Even so early in our relationship, Bobby and I were equal partners and we came together in prayerful consideration of his calling. 'The family that prays together, stays together' is an old saying but holds much truth. When a married couple can give themselves over to the Lord and allow their burdens to be lifted onto His shoulders, it is simply easier to cope with the inevitable obstacles which come your way.

We decided to sell our home and move to Minnesota so Bobby could attend the Apostolic Bible Institute in St. Paul. Once there, I decided to also take classes. It was a four year program, so we thought we'd live there until Bobby graduated and then look for a pastorate, but once again God had other plans.

Bobby had forgotten to notify the draft board we had moved and he would be attending a different college. Since Centenary was required by law to alert the government when a male student of draft age left school, Bobby received a notice to appear before the local draft board in Louisiana.

We went back and Bobby took proof of his enrollment in the Bible college, but the members of the draft board were a little rough back then and one of the men called Bobby a coward and even threatened him with jail.

None of that was legal or enforceable, of course, but it incensed Bobby and he enlisted on the spot. Bobby could be stubborn and just decided to show them what he was made of. It was a quick decision that would have great import on both our lives. I firmly believe God had His hand in things that day, and used those men and Bobby's headstrong reaction to nudge us both toward the place He wanted us to be.

Without a bachelor's degree, Bobby entered the service as a private instead of an officer and was thus denied the extra pay and benefits he might have received had he waited until after graduation. This was unfortunate, but sometimes hardships serve to bond two people together, and that was the case in this instance.

While Bobby was in basic training in Fort Benning in Georgia, I took my old job at the electric company in Shreveport to help make ends meet. I prayed about what I would do while Bobby was in the service. We had only been married a short time and while I supported Bobby's decision it wasn't what I had envisioned for our first years together.

We spoke on the phone as often as we could, and he wrote me frequently. They were beautiful letters and when I read them I could imagine Bobby's gentle voice in my ear, sharing his innermost thoughts and emotions in such a way it only reinforced our love and commitment to each other.

I felt the Lord drawing us closer together during this time apart, and felt His guidance in my next life decision.

Bobby left for Europe in February of 1962, and I followed in August. I had decided to apply for a civilian position with the military. After passing the civil service exam, I was hired as a statistical analyst and assigned to the same base in Orleans, France where Bobby had been posted. The work I did then was much like the work I would do many years later in Baghdad. It was the first of many instances over the years in which my father's insistence I attend business college proved beneficial.

I was even awarded top secret clearance because I dealt with classified data, and Bobby and I shared many a laugh about my 'elevated' position of trust by the military.

Some men, especially as young as Bobby was then, might have taken offense or been resentful, but he was never so insecure. He was confident in himself and had no problem supporting me just as I supported him.

Looking back years later, I realize how far 'ahead of his time' Bobby actually was. Just as my mother had always assured me there was nothing I could not do, marrying a man who treated me as an equal at a time when many did not hold such views reinforced in me the confidence I would carry throughout my life, and which enabled me to go to Iraq as a grandmother in my sixties.

Both he and my mother were brave and bold in their own ways.

Bobby and I had our share of disagreements, but we never let the sun set on an argument, and our marriage was a real partnership. He always considered my opinion and I showed him the same respect.

We were bound together in love for the Lord and an adventurous spirit, and looked at this enterprising time as an experience to be savored.

What seemed like a bad deal when Bobby faced the draft board, later worked to the glory of God when Bobby began to hold services on the base in Orleans, almost from the day we arrived.

The two of us were eager to follow the path we felt the Lord had laid out before us, but we quickly learned never to take anything for granted.

When Bobby was first called to minister, I promised to support him in that endeavor. But neither of us knew then the way in which God planned to use him.

Bobby Dykes served the Lord, and his country, and he never took the easy road. And I was right there beside him. Right where the Lord wanted me to be.

9

IN SPIRIT AND PURPOSE

Humility

³Do nothing out of selfish ambition or vain conceit, but in humility consider others better than yourselves. ⁴Each of you should look not only to your own interests, but also to the interests of others.
Philippians 2:3-4

My son, Byron was scheduled to touch down in Baghdad a week subsequent to my arrival, and after those first chaotic days I was really looking forward to seeing him. Just the thought of my youngest child's smiling face did my heart good.

Everyone who entered or left Baghdad came through the transit center, which was actually just two trailers pushed together on the west side of the camp. There was an additional trailer next door with military style bunks for those required to stay overnight while processing in or out of the country, but fortunately this would not be the case for Byron.

The transit center was always bustling as one might imagine, with contractors leaving on and returning from R and R's (rest and recuperation) constantly. I had been so grateful Sharon was waiting for me when I arrived, and I wanted to do the same for Byron. Even though I had spent only a week in country, I still wanted him to benefit from my experience thus far.

I had not yet been assigned a vehicle, so Sharon arranged to use a car and we drove to the center to pick up Byron. I was eager to show him around the camp and hear all about his trip.

It is quite an ordeal to leave your home, train for weeks in Houston, travel to Dubai, spend the night in a hotel room with complete strangers, and then fly into one of the most dangerous regions on earth, all topped off with a corkscrew landing in case any insurgents decide to send a surface-to-air missile your way.

When you finally arrive at the transit center it feels like a lifetime has elapsed and you have already accomplished a great deal, and yet your work hasn't even begun. I wanted to help Byron adjust in whatever way possible, even as I was still struggling to do the same.

When he stepped off that small, dusty bus from the airport and saw me standing there, we both literally burst out laughing. Who would have thought we would ever share such an experience?

At that moment I could see in him his father Bobby, who was always so courageous and intrepid and joyful, and my laughter turned to tears. I had never been as proud of my son as I was at that moment. Byron was so young when his daddy died, but he was becoming more and more like Bobby with each passing year. It moved me so to see the man he'd become. Everything his father wanted for him, everything he wanted Byron to be but never lived to witness, was encompassed in that single, sweet moment. And then we were hugging and the moment became memory. My heart is filled with such moments and I thank God for each one of them.

Sharon drove us around to see the palaces and other buildings which were such a striking contrast to the many groups of dusty trailers scattered around the construction sites. I thought it was important for Byron (or anyone) to see some of the beauty of the surrounding area before getting down to work in the ugly areas filled with construction trailers and the like.

Five minutes away from the transit center and one could see many palm trees and flowers still growing even though the irrigation strips were no longer operating. The flowers would soon die, but then it was still possible to imagine their beauty at the height of the care they once received.

We drove by Victory Palace, where the top commanders had offices, and showed him the building across the surrounding manmade lake where General George Casey, Jr. stayed. He had replaced General Sanchez as the Commanding General of the Multi National Forces a few months earlier. General Casey's father was killed in 1970 in a helicopter crash while commanding the First Cavalry Division in Vietnam when his son was in his twenties. I can't help but think such an experience made General Casey a good choice with whom to entrust our young soldiers.

There were several smaller compounds around the palace area. Some of these were used to house coalition forces, who always seemed to get the best housing available when compared to American troops. I suppose it's the equivalent of allowing relatives to take the bed while you sleep on the couch.

The Australians in particular had a beautiful structure, complete with an Olympic-sized swimming pool. Months later, I watched as an Iraqi translator was baptized at sunset in that same pool as helicopters flew overhead and the warm desert winds blew across the waters. It was just one of many truly amazing experiences the Lord blessed me to witness while I was in Iraq.

We also showed Byron the little building in the middle of the lake where Saddam was being held. It was supposed to be a secret, but it was somewhat amusing that everyone always seemed to know where he was. If you ran into someone and got to talking about him, invariably the person would lean in close and whisper, "Don't tell anyone I told you, but..." and divulge the secret holding place where the former dictator was being kept until his trial. People are always people, I suppose, no matter where you go or what you're doing.

After the tour, we took Byron to meet his supervisor. Byron was hired as an MWR coordinator, but was quickly promoted to technician, which was one step below supervisor. He was assigned to Camp Striker, which was basically a tent city because so many troops rotated in and out of there.

Many would spend their first six to eight weeks at Striker before rotating out to other areas.

We left him there and I went back to work with a heavy heart. I didn't really know how much time I would get to spend with him in the coming weeks and months. As I said, I had been working at least twelve hours a day and had not yet been assigned a car, so I was unsure how easy it would be to coordinate our schedules to spend time together, which I had been hoping for. Even though Striker was nearby, it would likely take some doing.

I prayed that night for the Lord to bless Byron and keep him safe above all, but I also asked Him to provide some way for me to see my son at least a few moments each day. "That's all I ask, Lord. Just a moment or two with my son."

The next day, Byron was returned to Camp Victory because of a lack of space at Striker, and for sleeping he was temporarily assigned a room in a trailer just a few rows from me. During our time in Iraq we often were able to visit for a few minutes at the end of a long day's work. What a wonderful answer to my prayers!

We both began to settle into our routines, though mine was in flux for awhile when my department was dissolved.

Byron was assigned to the recreation center and gym at Camp Striker, which were located in large tents with small sections reserved for internet access, television, foosball tables, and other such activities. He worked with the officers coordinating special events for the troops such as five and ten kilometer runs, karaoke nights, and various sports and game competitions.

Byron owned and operated Holy Roller Skate Park back in Shreveport so this was right up his alley. He had always loved sports and games so we were both pleased he could work and contribute in such a way.

Later on he even bought a bicycle and would often ride out to the abandoned Baath Party Recreation area a few miles away and skate-board in the cement areas after working a full day. I worried about him out there all by himself, but I suppose it was a good way for him to relieve the stress of long hours and constant danger. He kept me mollified by promising to always keep his supervisor informed as to his plans.

No matter how old they get, your children can always manage to add a few grey hairs. But the Lord kept him safe and the thought of him nearby was always a great comfort to me.

Byron also had a serious side borne of losing his father at such a young age. A boy naturally becomes very protective of his mother in such situations, and both he and his older brother Bren were no exception. Both boys bonded strongly with my second husband, Bob Chriswell, who was as kind and loving a stepfather as I could have ever hoped to find for my sons. When Bob passed away years later after a long illness, Byron in particular took great comfort in being able to be there with him and take care of him in his final days as he could not do when his own father died.

Seeing Byron daily was a constant reminder of the two wonderful husbands and two equally wonderful sons I had been blessed with over the course of my life, and even during the roughest days in Iraq I praised the Lord in my heart for His bounty.

Some of the most trying times were when I was shuffled around for weeks after the logistics office was dissolved. In addition to incoming mortars and running to the bunkers and everything which goes with living and working in a war zone, I was very unsettled in my job. It was a very trying time for me.

Then the Director of Logistics told me that an MWR deputy manger position would be opening up in a few months. He decided to put me up for that position, and in the meantime to assign me to the MWR facilities in two different camps so I could learn their operations from the ground up.

I was very excited at the prospect of increased responsibilities, not to mention the extra pay, but it would mean I needed to keep quiet about the possible promotion and subordinate myself to the supervisors at these locations, all of whom were in their twenties.

I must admit I have an ego like anyone else, and sometimes it was a bit hard to take orders from others so young and relatively inexperienced. I had been hired at a particular pay rate and was actually making far more than they, so it was a little humbling in that way, too. I felt the burden of my pay and wanted to make a contribution commensurate with the compensation I received.

But I accepted the fact I needed to learn how everything was done at each facility, so I made the best of things. As anyone knows who has been supervised by someone young enough to be your child, discretion is often the better part of valor.

And as always, what seemed like a difficult situation turned out to be a blessing.

I worked two months each at two different MWR facilities, named Division and Scorpion, and during that time I was able to spend quite a bit of time with the soldiers. It was an experience I would not trade for anything.

I played chess with many fine young men. They were always unfailingly polite and respectful. As I got to know them, certain soldiers began to come in specifically looking for 'Mom Evelyn,' sometimes just to talk or say hello.

We were told not to ask the soldiers about their missions or experiences. Many soldiers wanted to use the center to escape from their work, as a place to forget the difficulties of war and relax and unwind.

But others wanted to talk, and we were encouraged to listen if that was the case. I heard many stories over those chess boards I would hope fine young men such as these never again experienced. Sometimes a game would stop completely so great was the need a soldier felt to unburden his soul. I felt blessed the Lord allowed me to listen and pray for these young people.

One young man in particular was an avid reader. He would come in and find me to tell me of a particular book he was reading and ask me if

I would read it, too, so he would have someone to discuss it with the next time he came in.

His taste leaned toward science fiction, which is not at all my cup of tea, but I kept that to myself and read whatever books he requested. He was always so excited to hear I'd finished a particular chapter or passage, and his eyes would light up like a Christmas tree when he spoke of a particular plot point or character that he'd especially enjoyed.

The only book he asked me to read that I really liked was The DaVinci Code, which I enjoyed mostly because of the religious symbolism which played a major part in the story. Though much of the novel deviated from what I knew to be Biblically correct, I understood it to be a work of fiction, and was able to use the book to share my testimony with this young man whose knowledge of scripture was more limited than my own. God often presents us with opportunities for spreading his message in the most unlikely ways.

But whatever we were reading, the look on that young man's face when we met made every selection of our little book club for two worthwhile in its own special way.

Many of these young men were especially anxious and fearful before missions, and though some claimed bravado it was obvious that it was extremely stressful for everyone. I would always tell them I would pray for them, and over time they came to know this was not an empty promise.

Eventually many soldiers began coming in specifically to tell me of upcoming missions and ask that I remember them in prayer. They weren't allowed to be too specific, of course, but it was clear when they believed the danger was more pronounced than usual and I tried to always be reassuring and provide as much comfort as I could.

I knew some of these soldiers might not come back, and as difficult as it was, I rejoiced in the Lord that these young men were prayerful before going into battle.

The efforts to humble myself to take orders from the young supervisors of the MWR facilities paled in comparison to the humility I felt before

God as he allowed me to pray with these brave young men before their missions. No matter what age one attains God always has more lessons for us to learn.

I often quoted to these young soldiers the verse from 2nd Samuel 22:3, "My God is my rock, in whom I take refuge, my shield and the horn of my salvation. He is my stronghold, my refuge and my savior— from violent men you save me."

I will forever remember the faces of those soldiers and cherish the time I spent with them.

10
EMBRACING LIFE
Christian Adventure

*¹Therefore, since we are surrounded by such a great cloud of
witnesses, let us throw off everything that hinders and the sin that so
easily entangles, and let us run with perseverance the race marked
out for us. ²Let us fix our eyes on Jesus, the author and perfecter of
our faith, who for the joy set before him endured the cross, scorning
its shame, and sat down at the right hand of the throne of God.
³Consider him who endured such opposition from sinful men, so
that you will not grow weary and lose heart*
Hebrews 12:1-3

The first time I boarded an airplane I was twenty-one years old and on
my way to meet my husband, Bobby, where he was stationed in Orleans,
France. I was to make a short stop to attend the wedding of my cousin in
Indianapolis, and then fly on to Paris by way of New York City. Back then
flying was an event, and I remember I even wore a hat for the occasion.

It was the summer of 1961 and my 'firsts' seemed to be arriving one
right after another at a dizzying pace. I suppose at that age it may be true
for most, but as a young woman of that time I felt my life was wonderfully
glamorous and challenging and I relished seeing the world and serving the
Lord with my husband. It was an exciting time for us both.

Bobby had been in Orleans six months prior, and when he met me at
the airport in Paris we had been married a total of three years and been
separated almost a third of that time. Needless to say we were overjoyed
when we found ourselves together once more.

Whenever I see young couples reuniting at an airport I am always reminded of that special time in my life.

After taking my civil service exams in Louisiana, I sent my paperwork to Bobby in Orleans and he took it into the regional hiring center. While it was not certain I would have a job when I arrived, he was told there was a good chance something would be available for someone with my training.

I arrived in France, as they say, bright-eyed and bushy-tailed, eager to learn about the culture and experience new and different things.

I received a bit of culture shock almost immediately, as I witnessed several men relieving themselves by the side of the road on the way to Orleans from Paris. Some of them didn't even bother turning around!

Bobby was greatly amused at my introduction to this particular habit common to the agrarian French lifestyle in that area at that time, and I'm sure the shock registered clearly on my face. I also suspect he refrained from warning me in order to tease me a bit. This wasn't exactly what I had in mind when I imagined experiencing new things, but I had to admit it was different.

The parkway was lovely, with trees planted approximately twenty feet apart right next to the road. But looks can be deceiving. I was saddened to learn there were many traffic deaths along that particular route. It was common for American military personnel on leave to take that road to and from Paris, and there were numerous instances of soldiers rushing back to base after having had too much to drink. Whenever I noticed a gap in the line where a tree once stood, I would say a silent prayer for those who came before us, and those who would follow.

Orleans itself is a lovely town located about seventy-five miles southwest of Paris, in a crook of the Loire River, which flows northward to the city and turns west before emptying into an estuary on the edge of the Atlantic Ocean.

The population in those days was about one hundred thousand, with an additional twelve thousand American military and civilians and their families who lived and worked in the area.

It was basically a sleepy, provincial town whose most prominent claim to fame was that its inhabitants had been liberated from the English in 1429 during the 30 Years War by none other than Joan of Arc herself, whose image graced the center of town in the form of a large equestrian statue the Americans affectionately called 'Joanie on the Pony.'

A statue of someone named Dorothy LaFarge near one of the bridges which spanned the Loire was nicknamed 'Dottie on the Potty." Joan definitely got the better deal, if you ask me.

It was truly a magical time for Bobby and me in Orleans. We were young and very much in love, and getting to know each other as couples do, in that setting, was almost like a fairy tale. The farmhouses and surrounding countryside actually reminded me of the pictures in storybooks my mother read to me as a child.

In preparation for my arrival, Bobby had rented two rooms in a lovely two-story home owned by a French schoolteacher and her mother. Our bed stretched the entire length of our tiny bedroom and left just enough space for a wardrobe. The landlord slept just across the hall.

The house was surrounded on all sides by an eight foot stone wall and the lovely private yard was filled with beautiful flowers.

Our second room was utilized as a combination living room and kitchen, with two straight-backed chairs, a small table, and a hot plate for cooking. Old orange crates served as cabinets and the window ledge was our refrigerator. We had access to a bathroom down the hall, which had a small gas fired water heater we would ignite when we needed hot water. Each room had a separate oil heater which had to be turned off before we went to sleep. This led to some very chilly mornings and also gave our clothes a rather pungent odor.

As you can imagine, I often found myself explaining to new acquaintances the reason for the unusual smell, but almost everyone had such stories about their adjustments from living in the States.

Despite such minor inconveniences, Bobby and I had a wonderful time, using every moment to explore the countryside and drink in the culture. We both usually worked weekdays, and since Sundays were devoted to worship, on Saturdays we tried to plan something together or with friends to take advantage of our surroundings.

Bobby, of course, had made quite a few friends in the months prior to my arrival, so we never lacked for camaraderie on these excursions. Many of the military couples seemed to count the days until they were sent back to the States, but our attitude was the exact opposite. We were like children in many ways, always looking for new experiences and marveling at each discovery.

Initially we had no car, so often we'd walk down the narrow, cobblestone road from the house and cross the Orleans Bridge into town, where we might rent a scooter to ride through the countryside. Sometimes we'd explore the surrounding towns, visiting cathedrals and museums and speaking to the lovely townspeople who were always so kind to the American military personnel.

Even during our workday we found ways to enjoy each other and our surroundings. We would sometimes take a blanket and snacks during our lunch break to the banks of the Loire. In the evenings or on weekends, when we were not constrained by time, we might even take a book to read, or go to our favorite spot in the woods where a small creek flowed right across the road.

Toward the end of the month when money could get a little tight, we'd often simply play board games with our friends who lived on base, talking and laughing into the night. It was a nice break from our tiny quarters and we never failed to have a good time.

I think many of those without faith imagine Christians as dour and joyless, but with the love of Christ in your heart fun and laughter is always easily found.

On Sunday mornings we would worship in a movie theatre near the base. Bobby would teach the adult Sunday School class in the theatre while I taught the children in the boiler room. On Sunday nights Bobby would hold services on base, and many Friday nights we would meet with a French group for prayer and fellowship in a beautiful old building dating from the time of Joan D'Arc.

It was an idyllic time, to be so involved in spreading the Word in that setting, in that time, with each other. I can remember only a single disagreement the entire two years we spent in Orleans.

We were very active physically at that time; we were both young and strong and hiked up and down the road from our house sometimes several times a day.

After one particularly strenuous hike, I became suddenly fatigued and began bleeding. I was so young and inexperienced I had no idea what was happening to me, but it was very clear to the doctor.

I had suffered a miscarriage.

Naturally, we were devastated. We very much wanted children, and had I known I was pregnant, we would have taken greater care with my physical exertions.

The doctor advised me to remain in bed as much as possible over the next weeks, which of course I did. I tried to remain positive, but it was a traumatic time. There are so many emotions a woman goes through after such an event, and it was very difficult for me as a twenty year-old.

Years later, this experience would greatly help me when I worked as a counselor to young mothers. Praise the Lord for the wisdom He provides us even through tragedy!

Bobby was very solicitous, of course, and came home whenever he had the chance to bring meals to me and check on my well being. But he wasn't much older than I, and I suppose we both still had some maturing to do.

At the time, a possible deployment to Vietnam was on everyone's mind. The troop levels there, while nowhere near the heights later reached, had begun increasing at a rapid pace, so much so that the soldiers on base were advised to be ready to leave at a moment's notice.

Well, one afternoon, Bobby's prankster side apparently got the better of him, and he rushed upstairs and said in an animated voice, "The balloon has gone up!"

This was the code for an immediate deployment.

You can imagine the thoughts running through my head in that instant. Here I was, weak and on bed rest, believing my husband was to immediately leave for Vietnam. We had recently purchased a Volkswagen Bug which was loaded and ready for me to leave at a moment's notice with all our belongings in such a circumstance, and the implication for our lives at that point was staggering.

The thought of Bobby being called to Vietnam and leaving me at that time was simply terrifying to me.

I burst into tears.

The look on Bobby's face changed immediately and he told me he was only kidding.

Well, that was not my idea of a joke. I was angry with him for the first time in our relationship, and Bobby, seeing my reaction, realized he had gone too far. He apologized profusely, and I could see he felt very badly at the anxiety he had caused me.

Bobby was always a very kind person, but high spirited. He was a jokester. His outgoing, gregarious nature made him a naturally good preacher, but what made him grow into such a fine pastor was his genuine empathy.

But I think this was a real lesson for him, as it was for me. Even the best of us fall prey to poor judgment, and I know Bobby would have taken it back if he could.

That incident really stayed with him, and I believe, helped define the man he was to become. I forgave him, of course. Whatever punishment I could bestow was not nearly as bad as that he gave himself. Neither one of us ever could stay mad at the other for very long.

That incident proved cathartic, and as painful as it was at the time, actually helped us get through the loss of our first child. God will always find a way to teach us and strengthen us, and there is a blessing to be found in all things.

I soon got well and we resumed our routine, exploring our surroundings and each other, growing closer every day.

Our landlady was wonderful to us, often inviting us into her parlor for dessert and conversation. When Bobby and I returned to France years later as missionaries, we visited the schoolteacher, whose mother had unfortunately passed away by then. We had a lovely time reminiscing about our days in the house. Small kindnesses so often resonate in ways far beyond what we can imagine at the time.

Our years in Orleans were a wonderful, spiritually uplifting time, idyllic for two young people in love with each other and eager to serve the Lord.

I often look back on that period with amazement at God's wonderful blessings. Though we had no idea then our time on earth together would be as short as it was, by the grace of God, Bobby and I were living each moment as if we did.

Psalms 91:11 says: "For he shall give his angels charge over thee, to keep thee in all thy ways."

Angels were surely watching over Bobby and me in our first years together.

11
COUNTING MY BLESSINGS

Thanksgiving

16Be joyful always; 17pray continually; 18give thanks in all circumstances, for this is God's will for you in Christ Jesus
1 Thessalonians 5:16-18

One of the many things I learned from my experiences in Baghdad is just how much I have to be thankful for. Simply being born in the United States and having the benefit of the freedoms our soldiers were now attempting to secure for the Iraqis is something I don't know if I fully appreciated until I actually got my 'boots' on the ground.

And, of course, there are also the simple things in life which we as Americans can so easily take for granted if we're not careful. I truly believe our nation has been touched by God, and much is expected from those to whom much is given.

I tried to always remain conscious of my responsibility, not only as an American, but as a Christian, to set my very best example in all things.

I interacted with people from many different countries while in Iraq, and I could often feel a strong emotional response toward the Americans from those born in other countries. Sometimes it was curiosity, and sometimes it felt a little like envy.

Not necessarily in a negative way, more in the sense of yearning to understand what it was like to live in a country they had heard so much about, with such freedoms and opportunities they may not have experienced in their homelands. No matter how difficult things got, I always thanked the Lord for allowing me to serve Him and placing me on the path He'd chosen for me.

Having traveled abroad I was prepared for the difference in simple comfort unavailable in other countries compared to what we enjoy in the United States, and of course this was only magnified in a war zone. But beyond that I was constantly reminded of just how many blessings I have enjoyed.

Above all else is the fact I have felt the peace of God my entire life. Just knowing Jesus Christ as my personal savior transcends all else, and I was eager to share that with anyone who hungered for such things. But I also hungered myself for Christian fellowship.

One of God's gifts I never took for granted in Iraq is friendship. True friendship is a blessing and as a Christian I was always concerned with finding other like-minded individuals with whom I could praise the Lord. Psalms 133:1 says, "Behold, how good and how pleasant it is for brethren to dwell together in unity!" Simply being around others who love the Lord makes life so much easier. It is such a joy to find others who find joy in Christ, and finding Christian fellowship also helps keep you on the Lord's path for your life.

1 John 1:7 says, "But if we walk in the light, as He is in the light, we have fellowship one with another, and the blood of Jesus Christ his Son cleanseth us from all sin."

I found such fellowship with Shirley Booker.

Shirley was the MWR Regional Manager. She replaced Johnny Kelly, with whom I had established a good rapport in my job as logistics supervisor. Johnny was also from Shreveport, so we had the natural affinity of those with common homesteads.

But merely two weeks after I arrived in that office, Johnny was leaving Iraq to return to the States, so I was anxious to meet his replacement.

During my time in Iraq I always sought to work with others who loved the Lord. I had been shuffled around from place to place, with my duties changing and challenging me, but faith was my constant and I prayed the Lord would bless me with co-workers in whom I could find spiritual support.

I was not worried because God had brought me this far and never failed to take care of things in that regard.

Soon enough, Shirley and I had a personal conversation over lunch. We were close in age and found we had much in common, in particular our faith. It was such a strong component of both our lives it was a natural and easy transition to discussing our spiritual needs.

We had both been praying for a co-worker who loved the Lord, and we were so very happy and relieved to discover we each turned out to be the answer to the other's prayer! What a blessing she was to become in my life.

We quickly became great friends, bonding over stories of our lives and our families. Shirley is one of those people in whom I would trust my life; a person who could be depended on no matter the situation, in good times or bad.

Shirley restructured the office and made me her deputy, which meant we worked together quite closely. I shared an office with this wonderful woman for two years, and she made a tremendous difference in my life. She often told me she felt the same way about me. I'm not sure if either one of us would have been able to endure the difficulties of Iraq as long as we did without the other to provide love and support.

Whenever I got discouraged, Shirley would lift me up, and I'd like to think I did the same for her. Her faith was a constant inspiration to me.

Each day, no matter how hectic things got, she would take the time to hold a devotional over the phone with her husband back in Saledo, Texas. I would leave our little office and allow her a few moments of quiet time during which she would read the Bible and pray with him half a world away.

It reminded me of the happy times I had spent in Bible study with Bobby, and later with my second husband Bob Chriswell. I was blessed with two companions who loved the Lord. He is truly the glue that holds us together, husband and wife, friends and family.

As the hymn by John Fawcett and Walter Kimbrough says, "Blessed be the tie that binds our hearts in Christian love; the fellowship of kindred minds is like that to that above." Fellowship with other Christians is true fellowship with God.

Shirley also became friends with my good friend from the States, Sharon Gillis, who the Lord had first used to bring me to Iraq. We enjoyed many lunches, and even found time to shop together. Even in a war zone, we girls need to shop!

Shirley and I attended many, many Sunday evening worship services together. I can't stress enough how much richer my life is for having known this lovely woman.

When Shirley left Iraq it was a sad day for me, but I rejoiced in her friendship and thanked God that He allowed us our time together. I was happy she could reunite with her family and that her time there had helped provide the financial means by which she and her husband could realize their dream to open a little restaurant back home.

One day, if I'm ever in Killeen, Texas, I look forward to stopping in at Booker's Bar-B-Que and sharing a laugh and maybe a cry with my dear friend Shirley Booker, one of the many answers to prayer I received during my time in Iraq.

12
TO THE ENDS OF THE EARTH

Trust

⁵ Trust in the LORD with all your heart and lean not on your own understanding; ⁶ in all your ways acknowledge him, and he will make your paths straight. [a]
Proverbs 3:5-6

In the summer of 1963, Bobby and I decided to take a trip to the Holy Land. We planned to drive across Europe from Orleans to Jerusalem, taking the entire month of September as an extended R and R. We'd purchased a Volkswagen Bug the year before, and although our friends thought we were crazy, we were determined to make the trip to see some of the places we'd read about in the Bible since we were children.

It turned out to be one of the formative experiences of my life, and one whose effects I carried with me to Iraq forty years later.

We originally planned to travel by air because Bobby's father wanted to make the trip with us. He was to come to Orleans from the States and fly with us on to Jerusalem, but circumstances prevented that from happening. Bobby was relating this to some friends of ours one evening, and jokingly suggested he and I might just drive to Israel in our little Bug, instead.

Everyone laughed, but a few days later two of those present, Jim Plunk and John Morgan, advocated we all do exactly that, and they made us an offer we couldn't refuse:

If Bobby and I provided the car (our poor little Bug!), Jim and John would pay for gas and oil and the trip would be affordable for us all. They had listened to Bobby speak of the Holy land and his hope to visit one day and decided to turn his little jest of driving there into a reality.

Bobby said yes immediately, and after a tiny hesitation I was along for the ride. Literally. Generally speaking, I was a bit more cautious than Bobby, but his enthusiasm was infectious and before I knew it I was every bit as excited as he was.

Now, at this point you're probably wondering: What on earth is a nice, twenty-two year old Christian girl doing on a thirty day camping trip with three twenty-five year old, red-blooded American soldier boys?

Looking back, I have to laugh, because I suppose it was a bit unusual back then. But of course, one of those men was my husband, a man I had grown to respect more and more each day, watching him preach every Sunday, learning and growing and constantly affirming his commitment to Christ and to me as his wife and partner. Bobby was a man with a plan, and he was definitely going places. Places I wanted to be. I would have followed him to the ends of the earth. I trusted Bobby Dykes with all my heart.

As for the other two, they were both good Christian boys we had met through those same chapel services Bobby held in Orleans each Sunday. We'd become good friends in the Lord, providing the kind of good Christian fellowship every believer seeks. So I was comfortable traveling with them.

And of course, there was a fourth man with us, one in whom I had long ago placed my unwavering faith, and one who we all would have to trust for protection and guidance on this and every journey.

With Jesus in the car, I knew we would be okay.

As for our two earthly companions, Jim was a country boy and every bit the jokester Bobby was. They were like two peas in a pod. Jim would say some of the funniest things out of the clear blue sky in a very matter-of-fact way which sometimes caused me to wonder if I'd heard correctly before bursting into laughter. He and Bobby never failed to make things interesting, and they were quite a match for each other.

John was a preacher's son who'd strayed from the Lord as a young man but rededicated his life to Christ since his assignment in France, and had a more serious nature. His temperament was actually closer to my own than Jim or Bobby, and he possessed a more reflective sensibility. But we still shared many laughs on that trip and he was also wonderful company.

Some of our friends were predicting how many days would pass before an argument would make us want to 'put someone out of the car,' and they were only half joking, but I could see right away our personalities meshed and felt we would be well suited to such a trip.

And we were. We all got along very well, and there were no arguments at all. Maybe we were all just so young and eager to explore the world that no anger could possibly temper our excitement. We were adventurous souls with kindred spirits.

Now that we'd decided to actually make the trip, we began to formulate our plans. We would travel across southern Europe to Israel and return across northern Africa.

I gave our route and checkpoints for our contact stops to the military, as required of anyone traveling with my security clearance. We applied for visas, purchased extra gas and water cans and installed a luggage rack on the car. It was all happening very fast, but that was the way Bobby was. When he made up his mind to do something, he threw all his energies into the task at hand.

Bobby and I had barely three hundred dollars between us for the trip, which would cover twelve thousand miles over thirty days, so he scrounged for extra C-rations from every friend at every mess hall he possibly could. C-rations were commercially prepared meals for soldiers in the field or for when hot meals were unavailable.

C-rations were contained in small cardboard boxes holding individual items in cans. There were several types, and the specific items would vary depending on production dates, but they all included a canned meat item, a canned fruit, bread, or dessert item, and a foil accessory pack with instant coffee, gum, salt, pepper, cream, sugar, cigarettes, and a spoon. None of us smoked, but later on during our trip we would be very thankful for those packages of Marlboros and Pall Malls.

One case held twelve C-rations and four little can openers, which were nicknamed 'John Waynes' because the actor supposedly had demonstrated their use during a WWII training film.

Modern C-rations are called MREs, or meals, ready-to-eat. I had to laugh whenever one of the soldiers in Iraq claimed that was three lies in one name, although if memory serves my opinion of the C-rations was not so different. Still, a meal is a meal and we were thankful for whatever the Lord chose to provide.

Bobby was so successful in his search for C-rations it ended up being quite comical. While he and I sat in the front seat of our little VW Bug, Jim and John brought up the rear surrounded by dozens and dozens of C-rations. All you could see in the rear view mirror was two sets of eyes peering out of the boxes.

We put C-rations everywhere. On our laps, between the riders in back, even in the springs of the seats. They were in the luggage rack along with cases of Coca-Cola.

We had so many C-rations we limited ourselves to the bare minimum of personal items, believing it was better to take as much food as possible in case money was tight, figuring we could easily wash our clothes when needed. We limited ourselves to three changes of clothes per person, which, for a girl on a month long trip, was quite a sacrifice. Bobby teased me about it, but I knew he was proud of his wife 'roughing it' just like the boys.

To top it all off, Bobby made a sign which read 'Jerusalem or Bust' for the back of the car. We were quite a sight when we left Orleans.

And we were in for quite an adventure.

We left about ten o'clock at night on August 31, 1963, and Bobby drove most of the night. Our first stop was in Geneva, Switzerland, which was quite beautiful. We drove around Lake Geneva and took some pictures before continuing through Brig, a picturesque town on the Swiss-Italian border.

The mountain pass on the other side of Brig was quite a difficult drive, and more than once I silently wondered if our little Bug was up to the challenge. But when I looked at Bobby, he was so happy and confident my fears receded, although I certainly did offer up a silent prayer or two just in case.

But the easy banter of the three boys made the time go fast, and we shared much laughter as we crossed into Italy at the end of our second day. Only forty-eight hours and it already felt like we were half a world away.

Our friends Ed and Laverne Selstad lived in Vincenza, Italy, and we stopped there to have fellowship with them before we all piled into Ed's car and drove to Venice for an afternoon gondola ride. Even though we were with others, Bobby and I shared many romantic looks while we marveled at the unique sights in this one-of-a-kind city. We returned to stay the night in Vincenza before setting out the next day for Pisa and the famous leaning tower.

Our accommodations in Pisa were not nearly as comfortable as Chez Selstad, as the boys joked. We spent our fourth night sleeping on air mattresses in a parking area before cleaning up at a little gas station on our way to Rome.

We stopped and ate watermelon from a roadside vendor and looked out at the Mediterranean, which appeared impossibly blue. At that moment in time it was almost a sensory overload. The smell of the ocean, the taste of the incredibly sweet watermelon, the sight of the deep blue water, the touch of Bobby's hand against my own, the sound of the waves crashing against rocky shores. How much we have to be thankful for. What a beautiful world the Lord has provided us!

Rome was like no other city I had experienced. The sights, the sounds, the traffic!

We actually found Vatican City by accident, and while I made sandwiches the boys walked around the walls of the tiny city.

We ate lunch and found a USO office where we were directed to an inexpensive hotel where we could clean up before touring the Vatican and St. Peter's Basilica. It was so very beautiful. The Sistine Chapel was just enchanting, and Bobby and I rushed to identify all the Biblical characters so beautifully rendered by Michelangelo on its ceiling.

We stayed only the one night at the hotel and spent the next day sightseeing. Rome is such a beautiful city with so much to see it's nearly impossible to view everything on a single day, but we came as close as we could.

We even toured the location where the Apostle Paul was held under house arrest for two years while continuing to preach the Gospel of Jesus Christ.

That night we camped outside Salerno. It was decided I would sleep in the car and the boys would sleep outside. We shifted the C-rations to the front seats and I 'made camp' in the back. We were all exhausted and the boys fell asleep immediately. As I looked out at the starry night, listening to the faint snores of my traveling companions mix with the sounds of the night, I thanked the Lord for allowing us the opportunity to experience the wonders of His world and keeping us safe along the way.

We had supper at the Air Force base in Brindisi, which is located in the 'heel' of Italy's boot, and boarded a ship for the crossing to Greece the following morning. I had never really been a fan of boats, but the Mediterranean was calm and beautiful. It was during this crossing that Bobby convinced me a possible future crossing of the Atlantic would be just as peaceful. He neglected to mention such a trip would not be so calm during the winter, an omission which would lead to quite an eventful passage only a few months later.

We spent our first night in Greece near Corinth. I imagined we could be on the very spot where Paul preached to the Corinthians. On his second journey to Corinth, Paul spoke of the need for stewardship. This was the call Bobby felt to preach the Gospel, and Paul's letters to the Corinthians would guide us in our own work as missionaries in the future.

Camping under the stars, Bobby and I were struck by the words Paul spoke here over two thousand years ago, praising the spiritual commitment of the Macedonians in 2 Corinthians 8: 3-5, "For to their power, I bear record, yes, and beyond their power they were willing of themselves; praying us with much entreaty that we would receive the gift, and take on us the fellowship of the ministering to the saints. And this they did, not as we hoped, but first gave their own selves to the Lord, and to us by the will of God."

The Macedonians had begged the Lord to minister in His name. It was truly awe-inspiring to be in that place.

In Athens we also shadowed Paul, touring Mars Hill and the marketplace where he spoke about Christ, as well as the ancient Acropolis. Wherever we went, Bobby made sure we knew the history of the area, and our discussions were lively and fun. If we didn't know where to go next, or what to see, Bobby would always have a plan to keep us entertained.

Outside Thessaloniki, we nearly lost our entire luggage rack on an especially bumpy section of road, but fortunately there was no damage save a dent in the hood.

We met many interesting people along the way, including an Eagle Scout director who had dropped off a group of boys in Yugoslavia and was making his way back to Italy all alone. He was so starved for company he offered to drive all night with us caravan style if one of the boys would ride with him.

In Greece, there was an amusing old woman at a small gas station without electricity, who made a mistake totaling our bill for gas and was quite puzzled indeed when we came back a half hour later so Bobby could return the $1.62 she had cheated herself out of.

We saw shepherds and their flocks who could have stepped right out of the Gospel of Luke, and a band of Gypsies telling stories around a campfire. We even purchased ice from a donkey cart in Thessaloniki! There were so many memorable little episodes which constantly intrigued and entertained us along the way.

We toured the ruins of the city of Phillipi and the jail where Paul was imprisoned. A camel caravan and water buffalo were other firsts. We were like children, wide-eyed and amazed at the things we discovered.

Wherever we went in Greece the people were extraordinarily friendly. If we stopped the car, strangers would approach and ask us if we needed help or directions, often offering us food or water and inquiring as to our plans.

Just before we entered Turkey, we had another mishap with the car, and the luggage rack once again came loose, this time crushing our hood and giving us all quite a scare.

Fortunately the Lord was watching over us and our luggage was undamaged, as was the extra gas can we'd brought along. I was amazed we didn't lose a single drop of fuel.

But we were in the middle of a dark road at ten o'clock at night, so Bobby and the boys got to work securing the luggage rack. Bobby even was able to pound out the hood and not long after midnight (and a few wrong turns), we made it across the Turkish border. There were many soldiers guarding the crossing, so we drove into the country a few miles before pulling over so Bobby could get a little sleep.

We made it to Istanbul the next day and stopped at the army base there to eat and rest. Being in the Army we had been able to take advantage of the military installations as we traveled, which was a real convenience. I also checked in each time, as required.

Continuing through Turkey, we came across many more camel and sheep herds and I teased the boys, who were looking quite scraggly from not shaving. I said all they needed was a scarf around their heads and a course in animal husbandry and they could get jobs as shepherds. It was funny because as military personnel they were always expected to be clean shaven, and while they may have been enjoying their time away from the razor, I doubt they were ready to take responsibility for a few dozen camels.

Outside Adana we had our first flat, and as Bobby changed the tire we could hear the Muslim call to prayer over the city's loudspeaker system. The air base outside the city was the last one we would see for awhile, so we stopped for ice and continued, once more following in the footsteps of Paul, to Tarsus, where he was born and known as Saul before his conversion on the road to Damascus.

On Friday the 13th of September, we arrived at the border with Syria, but we were not allowed to cross at first. It was six in the morning, and the Turkish border guards did not arrive until seven. Once they arrived, we were told we could not cross without a carnet. A carnet, simply put, is a passport for a vehicle.

We gave the Turkish guards some of the cigarettes from the C-rations, and they became much friendlier. As I said, none of us smoked, but border crossings could be a little tense at times and those cigarettes really came in handy at that moment.

The Turkish guards agreed to let us cross without a carnet if the Syrian guards would accept us. The Syrian side of the border was lined with tanks and many unsmiling, armed soldiers. It was quite intimidating.

The guards demanded Bobby get out of the car. As he tried to explain we were just passing through Syria, two guards began to search the car. When one of them saw a box of C-rations marked with the insignia of the U.S. Army, he jumped back quickly, which caused the other guards to tense up and point their weapons at us.

The rest of us were ordered out of the car, and as Bobby desperately tried to diffuse the situation in English, the guards were yelling in Arabic and pointing their weapons. I don't have to tell you my heart was in my throat. It was very frightening, but finally Bobby convinced the captain to allow him to open one of the boxes.

It was a very nervous moment as Bobby carefully opened one of the C-rations to reveal the food inside. He noticed one of the guards smile at the sight of the cigarettes, so Bobby offered them up and opened more boxes, distributing cigarettes to each guard. From the looks on their faces, American cigarettes were quite prized.

Everyone was now a little more relaxed, but apparently the person in charge of issuing the paperwork we needed to enter the country had not yet arrived, so the boys were ordered back in the car to wait while I was taken to the guardhouse.

Bobby looked very worried as I was led into the small building by two of the armed guards. I tried to reassure him with a smile, but I think we were both extremely frightened at the uncertainty of the situation.

I entered the small building, which was occupied by several other guards, all of them armed and fierce-looking, and none of whom spoke any English. They were laughing when I walked in, and it was obvious they had been talking about me.

I tried not to let the fear I felt show on my face, and prayed Bobby would also remain calm outside. Though very uncomfortable, I made an effort to communicate with gestures and smiles, and eventually realized their intention in bringing me inside was to provide me with a more comfortable place to wait. Afterwards, Bobby and I often spoke of how ironic it was that while I was trying to converse with these men, eventually even sharing a few laughs, Bobby was absolutely worried sick outside in the car.

Finally, the needed official arrived, and it was decided we would be allowed to drive across Syria to Lebanon as long as we took one of the Syrian border guards with us to ensure we didn't sell the car. The man joked we could always remove our tents and stay awhile if this solution wasn't to our liking, so we had no choice but to agree.

So now John was in the passenger seat as Bobby drove and the guard was next to Jim in the backseat. Yours truly found a pillow and rode uncomfortably all the way to Lebanon on the emergency brake. The guard spoke no English at all so he looked a little puzzled at first when we got the giggles at the absurdity of the situation, but after awhile he shared a laugh with us in spite of the language barrier.

When the guard got hungry, he rubbed his stomach and pointed to a ragged looking tent at the side of the road. Bobby pulled over, and believe it or not, that tent was actually a drive-in restaurant. A restaurant whose other patrons had all arrived by camel or donkey. There were no seats, so the diners just squatted in the dirt as their sheep grazed outside the flaps of the tent.

After seeing the large number of flies swarming around the food being prepared, we politely declined the guard's hand signal invitation to dinner and waited in the car while he ate. I was grateful to get a short break from that brake.

When we finally arrived at the border, the Lebanese authorities would absolutely not let us cross without a carnet, and the lure of American cigarettes would not sway the border guards as it had the Syrians, so it looked like we would be delayed a day or so.

Now we took a Lebanese guard with us to Beirut, left our car with customs, paid for the guard's bus fare back to the border, and checked into a hotel completely exhausted. I can't tell you how good a hot shower and comfortable bed felt after crossing Syria on the parking brake of a 1962 Volkswagen Beetle. (I wonder how many people could write such an improbable sentence?)

Bobby got up early the next morning, on Saturday, to get the carnet. Unfortunately, he was told there was no crossing stamp available until Monday. It seemed to be one thing after another, now. We were trying to conserve funds and couldn't really afford another night in the hotel, so we took a cab to the customs impound area near the docks to see if they would allow us to sleep in the car.

Bobby was a little angry at all of our delays, but overall things had gone so well on the trip thus far we weren't too discouraged. We had, after all, fully expected there to be some complications along the way.

We weren't able to get our paperwork stamped for crossing, and were told we could not stay with the car overnight, so Bobby asked if we could at least collect some of our belongings from the trunk.

When we got to the car, Bobby told us to get in. This was completely unexpected but we did as he said. When Bobby took charge, he really took charge, and we were all so surprised no one even thought to argue. As we drove toward the gate, Bobby ordered us to duck down in case there was any shooting, and calmly smiled and waved to the shocked guard as we passed.

My heart was practically pounding through my chest, and after we drove a half mile or so we sat up and just looked at each other in amazement and relief. The Lord was truly watching over us!

We found a nice camping spot on the beach outside of town. Bobby planned to try and find someone who could stamp our papers the following day, so there was nothing to do but enjoy the evening.

It was a lovely night and I cooked supper on the beach overlooking the sea as the lights of the city twinkled in the distance against the mountains. We set up our mattresses and Bobby and Jim went swimming in the Mediterranean while John and I talked and laughed about the previous day's adventure. As much as I had enjoyed the creature comforts of the hotel, I could not imagine a nicer way to end the day.

On Sunday, we finally got our stamp late in the afternoon. Bobby explained to the official how we had 'borrowed' our car the night before and why, but the man just smiled and completed our paperwork to exit the country. I guess he must've found our exploits amusing, although they were quite harrowing to us at the time.

Years later in Iraq, during times of danger or uncertainty, I would often hark back to the entire experience and find reassurance that the Lord would continue to bless and protect me if I only trusted in Him to do so. "The fear of man lays a snare, but whoever trusts in the Lord is safe." - Proverbs 29:25.

We arrived at the edge of Jerusalem very early Monday morning. The area was mostly rocky desert, and we somehow strayed off the right road and found ourselves facing Palestinian soldiers with machine guns at the ready, backed up by Syrian tanks.

We were stunned and frightened, and suddenly heard Israeli soldiers running up behind us with weapons drawn, yelling at us to stop. Needless to say, it was an unbelievably tense moment.

This was just a few years after the Suez War of 1956, during which Great Britain and France joined with Israel in an ultimately unsuccessful attempt to overthrow the Egyptian president, Gamal Abd al-Nasser and take control of the Suez Canal. Multiple assassination attempts had recently been made against Jordan's King Hussein, and Ba'athists had seized power in both Syria and Iraq earlier that year, which led to the rise of Hafaz al-Asad and Saddam Hussein, respectively, in those two countries.

Just prior to our arrival, Syrian and Israeli forces had been fighting in the demilitarized zone north of the Sea of Galilee, hostilities which lasted for several days until a U.N. brokered cease-fire ended the skirmishes, and now three weeks later we found ourselves looking down the barrel of those fearsome tanks.

I could go on and on about the wars, assassinations, and conflicts in the region, but at that single moment we were just four twenty-somethings quite shaken to realize the magnitude of the danger we were in.

But the Lord, as always, was watching over us, and we managed to explain who we were and what we were doing and after a short time we were allowed to go on our way.

Needless to say, we decided it just might be wise to hire a tour guide to avert any more accidental adventures like that incursion into no-man's land, so we inquired at the American embassy. An official arranged for a guide, a wonderful Arab man who we were surprised and pleased to learn had previously guided several visiting Pentecostal ministers.

He had actually taught Arabic to Reverend William McFarland of Marion, Indiana, whom Bobby and I both knew of and whom the United Pentecostal Church was sponsoring to build a church in Jerusalem!

What a pleasure it was to discover such a connection. It only served to remind us all, that God takes care of those who trust in Him and seek

His path. Our trip was truly blessed, and this was yet another example of His love and protection.

We saw the Dome of the Rock, where Solomon's temple once stood and where Abraham offered his son to God as proof of his devotion. We toured the Mount of Olives from which Jesus often prophesied, and at the base of which lies the Garden of Gethsemane, where Jesus prayed and sweat drops of blood the night of his betrayal.

The graves of Mary and Joseph, the Garden Tomb, Old Jerusalem; it was all so overwhelming to feel the presence of God and walk in the footsteps of His precious son and those who followed Him so long ago.

On our last night in Jerusalem, our guide took us to a particular restaurant where King Hussein was known to dine. It was beautiful inside, with colorful silk cascading down the walls and very low tables, around which were large, soft pillows for seating. The guide ordered our food, and we all felt like players in one of those old Rudolph Valentino movies.

Toward the end of the meal, several armed security men passed through the room and our guide whispered to us "King Hussein will be coming." Sure enough, a short time later the king walked through the room and entered a smaller, private dining area. I think our guide was very happy to have provided us with such a unique experience.

During our time in Jerusalem, he was very helpful and eager to please, and his knowledge and experience was a blessing. And though he was of a different faith, the Lord was able to use him to facilitate the deepening and strengthening of our own. Mysterious ways, indeed.

Years later, this same Arab man invited me into his home to share a meal with him and his wife when I returned to Israel.

Before I met him in the fall of 1963, I was mostly ignorant of his culture and admit I found Arab customs and the men in particular to be a little frightening. But his patience and kindness as our guide reminded me then that all God's children are precious in His sight, and that experience, which led to our friendship in later years, fed my desire to reach out to others of different beliefs during my time in Iraq.

Some time after Bobby's death I discovered my Arab friend had been killed in one of the many military actions that have plagued the region, which saddened me greatly. But his gentle spirit was a warm memory and informed my actions during the time I spent in Baghdad, serving as a reminder of our greater purpose there.

We decided to alter our plans and retrace our route home instead of returning across North Africa because passage from Beirut to Cairo was more expensive than we had anticipated. It was probably for the best as we were all pretty worn out and the more familiar route would likely be a bit easier on all of us.

We did decide to cross Bulgaria instead of Greece, a route which would also take us through Yugoslavia and Northern Italy. This was a little scary because I obviously had not notified anyone in advance we would be taking that route, but we put our faith in the Lord and vowed to be even more careful during this time.

We were still eating our C-rations, although we did give some to two boys riding a motorcycle on their way to Hong Kong. My heart really went out to them. That trip sounded almost as uncomfortable as sitting on an emergency brake across Syria!

Our poor Bug also seemed to be getting weary. We were running on bald tires by this time, which were now going flat with increasing frequency.

By the time we got to Ed and Laverne's it seemed like ages since we'd been there. Ed was on an exercise but Laverne was happy to have us stay the night. In her garage, we found the sleeping bags we thought had been stolen while we were in Rome, and had a chuckle over that. We left the next morning as everybody was quite eager to get home to Orleans. Also, the temperature was dropping, and I didn't know how many nights I could spend camping in the increasingly cold weather.

Just before crossing the border into southern France, the car battery died, but the boys got out and gave the Bug a push start, and we were on our way once more. After all we'd been through on our trip to that point it was just another minor obstacle to which we gave barely a second thought. We kind of got our second wind along with the car, and we traveled down through Monaco and Barcelona for sightseeing before turning north and completing the final leg of our journey.

Several more flats, two new tires, and some very cold nights in the car, and we were almost home. When we stopped for dinner at the air base in Chateauroux about three hours south of Orleans, I overheard some teenagers whispering about the 'beatniks' at the snack bar.

It took me a moment before I realized they meant Bobby, Jim, and John, whose hair and beards were quite scruffy after nearly a month on the road. I had to tease them about leaving on a vacation with Beetle Bailey and returning with Alley Oop. Or, in this case, Oops.

We arrived home safe and sound, a month older but years wiser. It was a special time for us all, but for Bobby and me it was more than just an unforgettable trip.

Our journey through the Holy Land in the footsteps of Paul, who devoted his life to spreading the Gospel, served to deepen our faith and inspire us in our devotion to the Lord. It was certainly a fun trip, and an exhilarating time. But it was also a spiritual journey for Bobby and me.

There is a famous poem about a man who dreamed of walking along a beach, viewing the events of his life along the shore like episodes in a triptych.

When he notices the two sets of footsteps became one during particularly difficult times, he asks the Lord why He abandoned him during the hard times.

The Lord replies, "That was when I carried you."

Bobby and I were young and in love, and we loved the Lord. Time after time during that trip He picked us up in His arms and carried us when things were hard.

Our journey in the footsteps of the Apostle strengthened our determination to serve Him as Paul had, and we were even more certain in our belief we would spend our lives together doing just that.

The Lord blessed us in service for twenty-one years of marriage, and carried me through the terrible time after Bobby's death.

There is nothing we cannot accomplish, nor any burden we cannot bear, if we trust in the Lord and endeavor to follow in His footsteps.

13

A BAGHDAD CHRISTMAS

Salvation

*16 "For God so loved the world that he gave his one and only Son,[a]
that whoever believes in him shall not perish but have eternal life.
17 For God did not send his Son into the world to condemn the
world, but to save the world through him
John 3:16-17*

There were days leading up to Christmas of 2004 which were quite difficult for me. Since I had only arrived in November, I hadn't been in country long enough to accumulate any time off, and I was feeling a little down in the dumps about spending the holiday so far from family and friends.

It's such a special time of year, and I had always been fortunate to celebrate the birth of Christ surrounded by loved ones.

I was blessed, however, to have my son Byron and my good friend Sharon there with me. As I've noted, Christians crave fellowship with other Christians, and things would have been much more difficult without their support during this trying time.

I grew up in a loving family, and left their warm embrace only to marry Bobby when I was eighteen. The Lord blessed us with two sons and twenty-one wonderful years together. Two years after Bobby's death, I married another wonderful man, Bob Chriswell, and together we raised the boys, watching them grow up and start families of their own. I had many more years with Bob, but when he died it was really the first time in my entire life I was alone.

Of course, a Christian is never really alone, and I found comfort in my faith. I was also very blessed to be able to surround myself with wonderful family and friends at that stage of my life, and the holidays were always when I leaned on them the most. So, while I was prepared for that first Christmas in Iraq, I knew it would not be easy.

I was determined to make the best of things, but the stress related to my job and the general pressures of adapting to such a radical change in lifestyle were formidable challenges, indeed. My emotions are always heightened around the holidays, and sometimes the burden of my circumstances was quite arduous to bear.

When things are dark it reminds us that our relationship with Christ is so very important. Everyone experiences such times, and there is never any shame in feeling discouraged as long as we lift our voice to the Lord and ask for His guidance.

December 24th was especially difficult. I was having problems with some of my co-workers who could be rather coarse at times, and I lost count at twenty-four the number of outgoing rockets I heard screaming overhead. It was hard to concentrate and I was feeling a little lost. I took a moment near the end of my workday and asked the Lord to provide me with the strength to rise above the things which could dampen my spirits during that special time. It's always comforting to know that no matter where you are, no matter what you're doing, God is always available for a little 'heart-to-heart' talk.

It helped that several women with whom I worked, who were all feeling a little blue as well, simply decided not to allow such feelings to get the best of us. We were determined to lift each other's spirits. There is nothing like good Christian fellowship.

Someone had sent a small artificial Christmas tree from the States which we used to decorate a corner of the office, and just looking at that tiny tree made me feel a lot better. It reminded me of that little Christmas tree in the Charlie Brown specials my boys loved to watch as children. All it needed to light up the room was a little love and attention, and someone to remember the wonderful story it symbolized.

I was even more heartened when Sharon arrived with an invitation to a special candle-light service scheduled for that evening in Victory Palace.

We worked until about seven that evening (an early night) and then Sharon and I exchanged gifts in her room before heading over to the service. They were just knick-knacks we had each found while shopping in one of the little kiosks the military allowed Iraqi shopkeepers to set up on base, but simply the physical act of giving my dear friend a gift further lifted my spirits after a rough day.

From there we went to the Christmas Eve service and had a truly wonderful time. We were met outside by guards who pinned us with a colored ribbon which meant we were allowed into the large ballroom where the service was to be held.

Just inside the palace there was a large, fully decorated tree in the beautiful atrium, and we were as excited as children seeing Christmas lights for the first time. There was something about being in that opulent place, built by Saddam Hussein, and gazing up at the symbol of Christ's birth that filled my heart with joy. It was so improbable on its face but it felt so incredibly right, that I was moved almost to tears.

My anxiety and apprehension from earlier in the day melted away, and once more I was reminded the Lord had placed me right where I needed to be. It is wonderful how patient the Lord is with His children, with our doubts and need for reassurance.

The service was lovely. The chorus of side-armed soldiers, their rifles on the floor at their feet, was an amazing sight to behold. When they sang, the acoustics in that room, with its marble floors and twenty foot ceilings made them sound like glorious angels.

So many thoughts ran through my head during that beautiful service.

I thought of Bobby, and how proud he would be that I was there. I thought of my second husband Bob, with whom I had been blessed after Bobby's passing, and our Christmas traditions.

I thought of my son Byron, who was still on duty at that hour, but had followed his mother half-way across the world to watch over her. I thought of my other son Bren, who was taking care of things back home. I thought of my three blessed grandsons, safe and sound in Louisiana. And I thought of my good friend Sharon, who had opened my eyes to the possibilities of serving in Iraq.

It was as if all the things He'd given me over the years paraded across my consciousness, and I was overwhelmed with joy and love for the Lord.

And I thought of Christ, whose birth we were there to celebrate, and whose ultimate sacrifice made our very lives possible. What a wonderful blessing that service turned out to be.

At that moment I knew I wouldn't trade places with anyone on earth. At that place, at that time, with those people, was exactly where I was supposed to be.

There was an enormous wooden table which dominated the center of the room, shaped like a horseshoe and beautifully finished. I'm sure Saddam often sat at the center of that beautiful piece of furniture with his generals, discussing the actions which brought pain and suffering to so many over all those years he ruled Iraq.

And now the room was filled with Christians celebrating the birth of Jesus, our joyful voices raised in fellowship and praise! It was truly an awesome experience.

At the end of the service, as each person used their candle to light the candle of the person beside him, the warm illumination slowly grew until the room was bathed in a beautiful, lustrous glow. I was struck by the peaceful feeling emanating from the faithful in the room. I felt the presence of the Holy Spirit very strongly, and I know the others did, too.

It was a truly amazing night, one I will not soon forget.

What a wonderful way to spend my first Christmas in Iraq. What a wonderful way to spend Christmas, anywhere.

As I looked back on the day, I had to smile at my earlier trepidation. How could any celebration of the birth of our Savior ever be sad?

I awoke to more rain and mud on Christmas morning, but nothing could 'dampen' my spirits from the night before. Sharon and I were able to take a little extra time off to have lunch with Byron at Camp Striker.

Just seeing him for a short time made my day, and I know we lifted Byron's spirits, too. Just like the candles transferred the flame from person to person during that service, Christians transfer God's peace to others who love the Lord, which is what fellowship is all about. And the joy flows right back to you.

Byron was able to open gifts from family back home, and he enjoyed the time as we told him all about the beautiful service at Victory Palace.

That night, I was able to retire to my room a little earlier than usual, and I thanked the Lord for one of the most truly memorable Christmases I'd ever experienced.

14

RESTORING MY SPIRIT

Restoration

"The Lord is my shepherd; I shall not want.
He maketh me to lie down in green pastures:
He leadeth me beside the still waters.
He restoreth my soul:
He leadeth me in the paths of righteousness for
His name's sake."
Psalm 23:1-3

David, who worked as a shepherd for his earthly father long before he ever slew Goliath with help from his Heavenly one, definitely understood the importance of rest and relaxation, or what is known in the military and beyond, as R and R.

Those first three verses of the 23rd Psalm, one of the most well loved passages in the Bible, obviously meant a great deal to me, but especially so during my time in Iraq.

There's an old joke that goes like this: During a revival meeting, a preacher called on his audience to always remember that "Satan never takes a holiday." A member of the congregation is heard from the back, "Yes, and look where *he* ended up."

David spoke of the Christian need for rejuvenation, and I took full advantage of the R and R's available to me.

Contractors were allowed fourteen days rest and relaxation every four months. This basically meant ten days off with two travel days allowed on either side of the break. My first four months in Iraq had been very stressful, both physically (adjusting to the lack of creature comforts) and psychologically (job pressures and general duty-shuffling), so I was especially eager for the opportunity to 'recharge my batteries.'

There were those who left on their first R and R and never went back to Iraq, but I felt that the Lord had placed me where He wanted me and I was determined to get some rest and then jump right back in the thick of things. I've always been one of those people who don't like to leave business unfinished. I felt the Lord had more work for me in Iraq.

"The Lord is my shepherd; I shall not want."

When we trust in the Lord, He promises to provide for us. We will want for nothing. Of course there are things in modern society we desire, but those things are ephemeral. God has a plan for our entire lives if only we will remain steadfast in our faith. It's not always the easiest path, but it's certainly the most fulfilling one.

"He maketh me to lie down in green pastures: He leadeth me beside the still waters. He restoreth my soul."

God understands our need for recuperation. He knows we must replenish our spirit, and guides us to a place of peace and tranquility.

The Good Shepherd understands the need to restore his flock. And the Lord provides the spiritual rejuvenation we need to continue His work.

When I traveled home to Shreveport in February of 2005 for my first R and R, I certainly did find my spirit refreshed, but the peace and tranquility was just a tiny bit harder to come by.

Once I actually arrived home it was quite hectic, simply because so many friends and relatives all wanted to see me and hear about my experiences. My days were filled with the comings and goings of familiar faces, while the evenings consisted of dinners and other such gatherings and events. And, of course there were the countless errands which pile up whenever you're away from home for long periods of time.

It was almost like Baghdad without the bombs!

Of course, I'm exaggerating, but my schedule was similarly busy in terms of things to accomplish during my waking hours. Plus, because there's an eight hour time difference, I was also dealing with jet lag. Overall, I found myself sleeping very little that first trip home, staying up quite late and waking up at five in the morning each day. Before I could adjust to an even slightly more restful sleeping schedule, it was time to go back to Baghdad.

One of the things that made it hard to drift off was the noise. There just wasn't enough of it. It was simply too quiet for me to fall asleep. My son Bren joked he might have to hire a helicopter to hover over the house next time so I could finally get a good night's sleep.

It was a blessing that on my first R and R, I was able to travel with Byron and Sharon. Not only were we able to do a little sight-seeing in Dubai on each side of the trip, but it was wonderful to allow others to be the focus of some of the attention at the various events with family and friends once we were back in Shreveport.

It was such a busy time I was completely exhausted by the time I had to return. Still, in spite of these things the Lord provided me with the spiritual rejuvenation I needed, and I was truly excited to go back to Baghdad and complete my 'tour of duty.'

During my time in Iraq, I took advantage of eight R and Rs not only to return home to Shreveport, but to visit other countries. I feel blessed to have had such opportunities, and my life is a richer one for the exposure to so many other cultures. It has given me a greater appreciation for the great beauty and wonder which exists in the world.

When I was in Perth visiting my dear friend Ida, I was able to speak of my experiences in her church. I visited the place where Maori chiefs signed New Zealand's declaration of independence. Sailing in the South Pacific was like a dream come true.

When I toured the Greek Islands with Sharon and our friend Von, it was one of the most memorable birthdays of my life, notwithstanding the sandstorm which delayed my flight out of Baghdad, a fire at the Istanbul airport, and a bumpy ride on a cruise ship which brought back memories of my long ago Atlantic crossing with Bobby. And though Sharon and Von teased me at the time for my anxiety, the very same cruise ship sank a year later! (I nearly fainted at the news reports and my friends don't tease me any more)

I even visited with missionaries in Bangkok, and retraced my steps in Turkey from that long ago Volkswagen trip with three shaggy soldier-boys.

I even was able to time one of my R and R's to coincide with Daddy's 90th birthday celebration in Shreveport, which was a wonderful time.

Not long after I left for Iraq, my father had fallen off his scooter which he used to ride around the senior center and deliver newspapers to the residents. Actually, he was just picking up their papers at the end of the driveway and driving them up to the porch.

I was, of course, very worried at the time, but happily Daddy recovered just fine and so I was especially happy to celebrate with him at that age on one of my trips home.

As much as I loved my work in Baghdad, my time away was rewarding, as well.

Those R and R's were restoration for my soul, and what wonderful blessings the Lord provided me!

We must always remember the Lord wants us at our best, and understands our needs. Everyone requires rest to restore their spirit to do God's good work.

Most parents have, at one time or another, told their children, "I know you better than you know yourself." And so the Lord knows His children, their strengths and weaknesses, their limitations and their abilities.

Just as the Shepherd leads his flock to a place of rest and relaxation, the green pastures and still waters, the Lord leads us to place of solace; He restoreth our souls.

As I made the return trip to Iraq after my very first R and R, I was more focused than ever on my task and ever thankful to the Lord for bathing me in His love, filling me with His peace, and allowing me the opportunity to serve in His name.

15

FIGHTING FEAR

Protection

"Yea, though I walk through the valley of the shadow of death,
I will fear no evil: for Thou art with me,
Thy rod and Thy staff they comfort me.
Thou preparest a table before me in the presence of mine enemies:
Thou anointest my head with oil;
my cup runneth over.
Surely goodness and mercy shall follow me all the days of my life:
and I will dwell in the house of the Lord forever."
Psalm 23: 4-6

After rest, work; after work, rest. The Lord rejuvenates our soul and replenishes our spirit that we may better serve Him. He knows we are imperfect; we will falter, we will doubt, we will fear. But He is always with us.

There were many times while in Iraq, that I felt fear. Fear for my life, fear for the lives of others, fear that I was not up to the task the Lord had set before me. But God understands. He always found a way to let me know He was right there with me, to pick me up should I fall, to protect me from harm, to comfort me when times were difficult.

These feelings of fear were always fleeting, as I continually 'gave it up' to God and allowed Him to assume the burden of my protection. His peace is all powerful, and there was never a time I doubted He would come through for me if I continued to trust in Him.

My faith in the Lord and my complete trust in Him is a constant throughout in my life. It is what sustains me. It is what gave me the courage to travel to Iraq in my sixties, and it is what gave me the courage to stay until my time there was complete.

But there were some very scary times.

I've already related the story of my first bunker experience, which was frightening and quite a 'baptism' into the war zone. Such episodes happened with regularity. Incoming fire was a daily occurrence, often close enough to shake the modular buildings in which I worked and slept.

It took some getting used to, lying awake at night listening to the low flying helicopters and realizing these young soldiers were going out on missions from which they may or may not return.

The near constant sound of the helicopters and planes overhead, as well as heavy trucks and humvees on the roads in and around camp reminded me every moment of the dangers of being in a war zone.

The very first week I was there, an incoming mortar hit very near the DFAC as I was walking toward it, which was obviously a scary experience. One soldier was killed and two others were wounded walking from the PX (post exchange).

There were also times when the explosions were so close and loud that I dared not leave my room to run to a bunker, and the only thing I could do was cover my ears and pray. I did not always know if the rockets were incoming or outgoing, or even how close they were. There were nighttime attacks such as these which lasted for several hours, and the uncertainty could be very unsettling.

One day when I was working in the Regional Office, my co-workers and I heard a commotion just outside the door. We opened the door and discovered a man lying at the bottom of the steps between the trailers, bleeding. He had been shot. The trailers were very close together with wooden decks between them, and someone from the next trailer was already providing aid to the poor man.

Several days later, in that same cramped office, a co-worker sitting right next to me suddenly jerked in his chair and cried out "I've been shot!" A bullet had come through the ceiling and grazed his leg about eighteen inches from me. Fortunately, he was not seriously injured, but it was quite a startling experience! We learned later that several nearby offices were also hit the same day.

There was a time when fighting broke out just on the other side of the wall surrounding the camp, which was quite close to my office, and I wondered if the combatants would come right through the barrier.

Another time, some insurgents drove a truck right through a gate and briefly escaped for a short time into the camp.

One night near the end of my time in Iraq, as I worked late in the office, I heard a rocket hit very nearby. As I was reaching for my helmet and vest, a second rocket hit. I hurriedly got on my gear and ran outside toward the bunker. As I ran, I heard a low whistle right over my head and knew a third would soon hit.

I dove to the ground and covered my head just as the rocket exploded right past the bunker. As I lay on the ground, I spoke to the Lord and told Him I thought I might be coming to the end of my time in Baghdad.

I went back to the office with acute chest pain, took an aspirin, and sat in the dark until I could calm myself. I called the States and spoke to my son Bren. I just wanted to hear a familiar voice and to once again send a message to my family back home how much I loved and missed them. That incident actually led to my exit from Iraq some three years after I arrived.

There was always something going on which could overwhelm a person with fear, but experiences such as these encouraged me to remain constantly in a state of prayer and deepened my relationship with God. I always felt the Lord's comforting presence to calm me.

"Yea, though I walk through the valley of the shadow of death, I will fear no evil: for Thou art with me, Thy rod and Thy staff they comfort me."

Even with all these things going on around me, my fears were quieted by the knowledge He was right there with me every hour of every day.

"Thou preparest a table before me in the presence of mine enemies: Thou anointest my head with oil; my cup runneth over."

The Lord provided for my every need even as I worked in such proximity to insurgents on the other side of the wall who would do me harm. All the blessings of a lifetime's relationship with Christ came to bear and I felt overwhelmed by God's love.

"Surely goodness and mercy shall follow me all the days of my life: and I will dwell in the house of the Lord forever."

I knew without a doubt that the Lord would care for me as long as I stayed in Iraq and beyond. It is an almost indescribable comfort to know with certainty that a loving God is, and always will be, watching over you.

In this life and the next.

16

IN SICKNESS AND IN STEALTH

Perserverance

[16] Therefore we do not lose heart. Though outwardly we are wasting
away, yet inwardly we are being renewed day by day. [17] For our
light and momentary troubles
are achieving for us an eternal glory that far outweighs them all.
[18] So we fix our eyes not on what is seen, but on what is unseen.
For what is seen is temporary, but what is unseen is eternal.
2 Corinthians 4:16-18

In February of 1964, Bobby and I boarded a troop ship in Bremerhaven, Germany, bound for New York City. Crossing the North Atlantic during the winter is definitely not an experience for the faint of heart, and one which I certainly will never forget. Especially given my delicate condition.

Bobby's two year stint was up the following August, and we had spent many months praying about the future and asking the Lord to guide us toward His path for our lives. Bobby had, at one time, considered re-upping and becoming an Army chaplain, but our trip to Jerusalem really stoked his fire to get out in the world and preach the Gospel. Once he informed his superiors he definitely planned to leave the military, we were sent back to the States to finish out his time.

And so we found ourselves, as so often is the case in the military, standing in a very long line, waiting to board the ship.

After we returned from Jerusalem, I told Bobby I thought it was time to have a baby. We both had always spoken of starting a family, and since it appeared we would be settling down back in the States, it seemed like the time was right.

The first few years of our marriage had been a little unsettled, with several moves and months at a time spent apart, but now it seemed our lives were falling into place and we were eager to begin the next chapter.

Soon thereafter I was pregnant, and we were both deliriously happy. Not long after that, Bobby got his orders, and that was how I was separated out of another long military line with several other pregnant women to see a doctor and receive special instructions and Dramamine before the ten day voyage home.

I didn't think I needed the pills, and said so, but the doctor just smiled gently like someone who's heard the same thing many times before and told me I would not be allowed to make the trip without it. I acquiesced, even though I maintained it unnecessary.

I'm sure you have already guessed who was right in that particular disagreement. The entire bottle of Dramamine would be empty and I would ask for more long before we made it into New York harbor.

The enlisted men ate and slept in the hull of the ship, or "the hole." From the nickname you can imagine the difference in the officers' accommodations on the upper decks. While Bobby slept in a swinging hammock in the hole, I was assigned a small stateroom with a lavatory and a single roommate, also pregnant, several floors above.

Those on the upper decks, being officers, wore their civilian clothes, as opposed to the enlisted men below who were required to wear their uniforms at all times. We didn't like the idea of being separated, but any enlisted man caught on the upper decks was subject to a court martial, so we just determined to make the best of things. I didn't want Bobby to worry about me, so I kept my chin up and told him I would be fine.

However, I wasn't feeling so chipper after settling in. I was already feeling a little lonely, and while my accommodations were quaint, I missed my husband. Before long, the dining bell sounded, and since my roommate wasn't hungry, I glumly changed clothes and left for dinner alone.

There was, of course, a line to the dining hall. I could see a steward standing at the door handing out numbers to assigned tables, which would be in effect for the duration of the trip. It was just another reminder of the many meals I would be eating without my husband over the next ten days. I took a deep breath and asked the Lord to keep me strong.

The line was moving slowly, and just before I got to the entrance I felt a tap on my shoulder. It was Bobby! He was smiling and out of breath, and a real sight for sore eyes. Not to mention an answer to my prayers.

He'd changed into his civilian clothes and somehow snuck upstairs unnoticed, risking quite a bit of trouble to look after me. Needless to say I was happy to see him, but floored by his boldness. Although after our experiences during the Jerusalem trip, I suppose I should not have been surprised at the lengths he would go to protect me.

After the steward gave us our numbers for the same table, he guided me into the room and we sat down for dinner with six strangers, any one of whom could have reported Bobby had they known his rank. I was the only woman, and the others were very solicitous and genuinely seemed to enjoy the company of a woman at their table.

Bobby's natural gregariousness and ease in any situation came in handy during those meals; you might say he was the life of the table. More than once he was able to steer the conversation away from subjects which might have led to his discovery. Once, when one of the others asked him point-blank what his rank was, Bobby managed to change the subject, cause the entire table to laugh, and make the asker forget the question, all in the space of a few seconds. I had to marvel at his way with people.

During a particular meal, one of the officers at our table mentioned the rumor of an enlisted man who had been sneaking to the upper decks to take advantage of the superior dining facilities. Our dining partners all leaned forward, curious about the 'intruder.' Bobby and I were particularly interested, of course.

It was decided at our table that sentries should be posted at several locations in an attempt to catch the scoundrel. This information was also of particular interest to Bobby and me.

In spite of the danger, for each and every meal of that voyage, Bobby changed clothes without attracting attention on the lower deck, snuck upstairs without being noticed, and made it to the dining hall in time to hold my chair for me, all without missing a single meal. Who knew I'd married James Bond?

Bobby's presence turned out to be a very good thing, because the ten days of that voyage turned into fourteen due to some very rough seas. It was quite a change indeed from the peaceful, romantic crossing of the Mediterranean Bobby and I had taken only months before.

About three days into our trip, the storms started. Big storms. Three of them. One right after another.

It's difficult to describe the feeling of being on that ship in the middle of the Atlantic Ocean during a violent storm unless you've experienced something similar.

The entire bow of the ship would lift out of the water, vibrating as it rose. You could hear cargo in the hold below, sliding and crashing beneath you. Then the front of the ship would slam back down onto the water, very hard. This would happen over and over and over again.

Imagine the lurching feeling you get on a roller coaster at the moment just before you start downward on the first steep drop. Now imagine that feeling for hours at a time.

Everyone was given Dramamine once the storms started. I was grateful that I already had it in my system, but I can't say how much it helped me. I don't know where seasickness ended and morning sickness began. All I knew was that I was four months pregnant and I would have quite a story to tell my child about his or her first boat ride.

Spending time on a troop ship with no duties means your days revolve around mealtimes. I had books, but the act of reading only made things worse. Routine is what I had to pass the time. It was far from pleasant.

My routine was this: I would go in for a meal but tell the steward I could not eat. I would be told I must eat. I would eat what I could. Then I would throw up what I'd eaten. At the table. Into a bag. After which a very nice attendant would remove the bag, and hand me another.

And so it went. Every single meal.

It sounds embarrassing, but frankly, I was feeling so sick it would have taken too much energy to worry about it. My roommate had it even worse, and was unable to leave the room. Her meals were brought to her, and she suffered in private. I wanted to see Bobby, so I went to meals.

Several people had gotten injured during the first storm just walking around the ship, so ropes were stretched along the decks outside to grab onto, but there were still instances of broken bones and other injuries from falls almost daily.

The storms rolled in one on top of the other. As soon as it looked like a break in the weather, another would hit and the routine would begin again. It got so bad we dropped anchor several times, which extended the trip by days.

At night I would wrap my arms through the rails of the bed to avoid being tossed onto the floor. Every night I prayed for safety, and every morning I thanked God for getting us through the night.

Any time I was tempted to feel sorry for myself, I would remember studying in school the ocean passages of the first settlers in America.

I cannot fathom the hardships they must have faced. As hard as it was for me now, those pilgrims would have marveled at how good I had it. I suppose it's always the same, and a lesson we learn and relearn most of our lives. When times are tough, we can rest assured there were those who came before who had it even tougher.

During the third and last storm, I was in the shower when the ship's horn blasted three times, which was the call to abandon ship. The sound sent chills through my spine. I stood there in shock for a moment, and then hurriedly put on my robe and made my way to the lifeboats.

People were scurrying about the deck in an orderly fashion. There was no panic, just an air of hurried resolve. I looked around for Bobby, but of course he wasn't there. He was far below, and the enlisted men down there were assigned other routes to the boats, far from my own.

I got in line for a lifeboat and asked the woman in front of me what had happened. She told me the hull had cracked and we were taking on water. The ship was sinking.

My heart leapt in my throat, and all I could think about was Bobby. I asked the Lord to bring me peace and to keep my husband safe. My precious Bobby, who was down below. "Please watch over him, Lord," I prayed.

I was next in line to get into the lifeboat when I felt a tap on my shoulder.

It was Bobby! He had made his way around the entire ship to the other side and caught me just before I stepped off. He simply would not allow me to get into that lifeboat in stormy seas alone. He took me in his arms and I burst into tears.

Just as I was about to speak, to tell him how much I loved him, and appreciated him coming for me, it was over. The ship's horn blasted the all clear signal. Those who were in the lifeboats were helped back on deck.

They had been able to seal the area which took on water, and we continued our voyage. Everything after that was easy, relatively speaking. It was, to use the metaphor literally, smooth sailing. We passed through the final storm and sailed without further incident into New York harbor.

Well, there was one incident of note. When we finally docked in New York, I was met on the bridge by two of the officers with whom we had dined every day. They stopped to chat as I waited with my luggage for Bobby. The enlisted men below took much longer to debark than those on the upper decks.

They asked where my husband was, and I said he would be there soon. The two officers were gentlemen, and decided to wait with me. I didn't know quite how to discourage this, but I remember saying several times they shouldn't worry about me, I would be fine.

After several minutes, they insisted on helping me off the boat with my things. They carried my luggage down to the dock, and waited with me, chatting politely.

Suddenly, up walks Bobby, *in uniform*, shaking their hands and thanking them for helping me with the bags and telling them how great it was to meet them.

We quickly hailed a cab, saying our goodbyes and leaving the two stunned officers with the identity of the outlaw soldier who had been sneaking up to the officer's mess, as well as a funny story to tell their buddies back on base.

After that experience, it was almost forty years before I could bear to board a boat. I avoided even ferries, sometimes at added time and inconvenience. In the years Bobby and I traveled the country evangelizing, my fear of being on the water often added quite a bit of time to our travels, but Bobby always understood, and never once teased me about it. I found out much later that he had been sneaking some of my Dramamine during that crossing, all the while pretending to be my big, tough man, which was why I needed a refill from the ship's doctor long before we made it into New York Harbor, so I suppose he realized there was plenty to tease him about, also.

In 2006, while in Iraq and long after its release, I finally got the wherewithal to watch the movie Titanic. Like everyone else, I had heard about the film but could never quite work up the courage to actually see what all the fuss was about. I guess it's amusing that I had the fortitude to go to Iraq but not to watch an historical romance.

Anyway, I had seen practically every movie available to me while in Iraq, and so I decided to conquer my fear and watch it. It took two sittings, all alone, with frequent pauses to catch my breath, but ultimately I managed to enjoy it.

Or parts of it, anyway.

Some of it was a little racy for my taste, and of course the actual sinking was the worst for me. It was so realistic it took quite a while to get through that section, and half the time I covered my eyes like a school girl.

But I must say, the spirit of the romance reminded me of a certain enlisted man who, like the character played by Leonardo DiCaprio, refused to let anything stand in the way of his protection for the girl he loved.

17

MY BODYGUARDS: DAVID

Heroes

¹Be imitators of God, therefore, as dearly loved children ²and live a life of love, just as Christ loved us and gave himself up for us as a fragrant offering and sacrifice to God.
Ephesians 5:1-2

I am protective by nature. That is to say, I have always felt within myself a strong desire to look out for others. I also feel very strongly about service. Service first to God, then to others.

To protect and to serve may be the motto of many law enforcement agencies, but it's also my aspiration as a Christian, a mother, and a grandmother. Nothing gives me more satisfaction than sharing whatever knowledge or skills I possess to help those in need, and I thank the Lord whenever He allows me the privilege.

Any woman will tell you that nurturing comes naturally after giving birth to a child, and of course my years as a preacher's wife only intensified my calling to serve the Lord by serving His children. Ephesians 6:7 says, "Work with enthusiasm, as though you were working for the Lord rather than for people."

Going to Iraq was a blessing filled with such opportunities.

Yet, even though I went to Iraq in order to provide whatever service and protection the Lord saw fit to allow, as a woman of my age, I also, quite naturally, inspired the protective feelings of those around me.

My physical appearance alone made many of the soldiers I met very protective of me. They often told me I reminded them of their mothers and grandmothers, and this concern engendered a bond which gave me many opportunities to serve via my testimony. It also allowed me to not only pray with the soldiers and offer spiritual comfort in that manner, but to simply listen to them as I imagined their own mothers would do if they were present.

In this way, I believe the Lord enabled us to help each other in our appointed tasks, and truthfully I received as much support and sustenance from these brave young men as I provided.

The soldiers were not the only ones who 'watched out' for me. Two of my 'protectors' in Iraq were MWR co-workers, men who could not have been more different but whose dedication to their jobs and determination to help others constantly gratified and inspired me.

David Krischke was in his mid-fifties, a gregarious former college football coach who talked a mile-a-minute and could always make me laugh. He was working in Baghdad when I arrived, and in addition to his other duties, he drove me back and forth to my assigned location for weeks before I had transportation or Sharon to depend on for rides. I suppose you could say we carpooled for a few months, and anyone who's carpooled knows how nice it is to never worry you'll run out of things to talk about. When David was around that simply was not a problem. He was a bit like Bobby in that sense.

But David lived life a little rougher than I was used to, and while he was always very respectful, he enjoyed teasing me a bit with stories from his past designed to make me blush. He was very colorful, and got along exceedingly well with the young soldiers, who reminded him of the boys he coached during his football days. He was always on the go, eager to take action to solve any problem which presented itself, sometimes even before a proper course of action could be determined.

I remember more than once, running outside to catch David after he'd heard a snippet of conversation about an issue at another site and rushed off to fix the problem before his supervisor (me) had decided on the best solution. He was always champing at the bit to help out wherever he could.

David really was quite a character, one of those truly memorable personalities. He would often go out and bring meals to Shirley and me from the DFAC, just to save us the walk to the dining hall in the overwhelming heat. He also knew of the injury to my foot, and went out of his way to save me from over-exerting myself if he could.

That was just one of many small kindnesses he performed without a second thought, for myself and others, and we became very close during my time in Iraq.

Just before Shirley Booker left Iraq, David accompanied her on a helicopter inspection tour of several MWR facilities in other camps.

When the helicopter took evasive action to avoid sniper fire, Shirley was very grateful, indeed, that David had been with her during that wild ride, and vowed she would never travel outside her home camp again.

David teased that he'd never seen eyes so large as Shirley's, but of course he'd been scared to death, too. Those helicopter rides were really something!

David was the co-worker who was sitting knee-to-knee with me in the modular office when a bullet came through the ceiling and grazed his leg. We had a laugh about it later because, since David had so much energy and could barely sit still, we marveled at the remarkable skill the shooter had displayed in hitting a moving target.

He used to trade e-mails with his wife every day, and said he enjoyed that type of exchange even more than phone calls. I thought that was odd, and asked him why he preferred written communication to verbal. David explained that, while he loved to hear the sound of his wife's voice, he loved her writing even more because he felt like he was getting to know her in a completely different way.

I thought that was lovely and quite romantic.

David had quite a harrowing experience while in Iraq, (not at all surprising), but one which couldn't help but make me respect him even more. Many people would have left immediately after surviving such an intense event, but David stayed on.

While being escorted back to Camp Victory from Forward Operating Base Rustamiyah in eastern Baghdad, the convoy in which he was traveling came under heavy attack by insurgents using small arms fire and RPGs.

Keep in mind David had been repairing treadmills at the MWR facility for the soldiers only hours before, and this was his first trip outside the wire!

David had been scheduled for a two day trip to the base to service the machines, but the roads had recently become so dangerous between the base and Victory that he ended up staying six days.

Baghdad is a very large city, but if you can imagine not even being able to safely travel a few miles from the suburbs of a large city into the downtown area, you get an idea of the level of danger even on short trips.

It was a truly frightening situation, and indicative of the tense atmosphere both soldiers and civilian workers lived under.

The insurgents were pushing in as close as they could, and they had recently been attempting to capture Americans, some of whom had been executed on video which was distributed to the media and over the internet. It was a very scary time.

Convoys were constantly being attacked, on top of the normal danger of IEDs, and the road conditions quickly went from green to yellow to red to black, which meant no travel was allowed at all.

Once things were deemed "safe" enough to escort David and the MWR team back to Victory, the convoy left the confines of Rustamiyah at 5:00 A.M. on the morning of December 2nd, 2004, which also happened to be his son's birthday.

David and the other five civilians had been briefed on what radio frequency to use in the event their vehicle became incapacitated, hit by an IED, and every other possible scenario, none of which were very comforting.

The last scenario they told about was an 'Alamo' situation.

An Alamo situation obviously meant no one was going to live, that the convoy had sustained such injury or damage that the insurgents would overrun them.

The sergeant giving the briefing told David and the others that they would be on their own in that case.

At that point, David told me, everyone was quiet for a moment, and then the sergeant told them, in that case, they would each need to make a decision for themselves.

They would need to decide if they would be captured.

Obviously, those horrible videos were on all their minds.

If the decision was not be taken captive, then the person would need to look for the nearest soldier, alive or dead, and secure a weapon to 'take care of' yourself, the understanding that you could either shoot yourself in the head or go down fighting.

This was quite a thing to contemplate as David's up-armored Suburban left the base with two Humvees in front, and two in back.

Once they got outside the wire, they were met by two Iraqi police cars, which would accompany them on the trip back to Victory and hold traffic when needed.

The convoy traveled mostly on an empty six lane highway, traveling at 70 miles an hour or better, except when going under an overpass, when evasive measures were taken to avoid any fire from above.

One Iraqi police car traveled in front, and one behind.

The police car in front pulled a half mile ahead for some reason, and just as the convoy rounded a curve they heard an explosion and came upon two vehicles, one the Iraqi police car, that were torn apart as if there had been a horrific crash.

But David and the others knew there had been no accident.

As the convoy passed, one of the Iraqi policemen was standing in the road, dazed, as his arm twisted in the wind.

The convoy quickly passed by the carnage and jumped the median to turn back and help.

As soon as the convoy stopped and two of the soldiers ran to help the wounded Iraqi policemen, insurgents began shooting at them from all sides. It sounded as if a hundred people were hammering on the vehicle.

The Humvee to the rear quickly had all four tires shot out, and a rocket had pierced its front, destroying the engine. Then an RPG was fired over the top of David's vehicle, missing by only a foot and landing in a nearby soccer field.

As children from the surrounding neighborhood ran out into the field to see what was happening as only children would do, David witnessed terrible carnage through the windows of his vehicle.

The other occupants were hysterical, but David managed to communicate to the driver that the car needed to be moved off to the side to a safer position.

A child was ten feet away from David at that point, and their eyes met briefly through the bulletproof window. He thought the boy might have been an insurgent, until the child gave him a tentative thumbs-up, which David returned as a sign the passengers were all okay.

Moments later David witnessed the death of that precocious boy to sniper fire after he had bravely attempted to help one of the dying Iraqi police officers.

The convoy eventually managed to escape the fierce attack and were met by two American tanks which escorted them to Camp Falcon.

Apparently there was an expectation of a large insurgent attack on that facility so there were plenty of heavily armored vehicles at the ready.

I have left out quite a bit of what David witnessed that day because it is too horrific to describe, but every coin has two sides, and he also saw much heroism.

Once the convoy was able to start up again, they were even able to leave the two injured policemen with some neighboring Iraqis for care before continuing.

The entire convoy was saved by the courageous actions of several members of the 177th out of Ohio, in particular a brave soldier named James Vanderpool, who had been the first to rise up and man one of the Humvees' turrets to return fire.

When the convoy finally made it to Camp Falcon, David saw bullet holes all around James' position in that turret, but he kept firing and was never hit.

David told me that from the looks of that turret, it seemed as if James was Superman, that nothing could touch him.

But I know who was protecting that heroic young soldier.

I spoke with James on occasion in the MWR facility, and he was yet another reminder to me to always give the soldiers a smile and whatever encouragement I could, though it hurt my heart to know what he'd gone through.

There are so many like him, so very young, just doing their job and helping protect our nation and the ideals and freedoms we so often take for granted.

James Vanderpool received a Bronze Star for his actions on that day, and because of his bravery, my friend lived to see another day.

You might say that soldier was my bodyguard's bodyguard.

And of course, the ultimate Bodyguard was watching over them all.

18

MY BODYGUARDS: KIRK

Authorities

[22]Slaves, obey your earthly masters in everything; and do it, not only when their eye is on you and to win their favor, but with sincerity of heart and reverence for the Lord. [23]Whatever you do, work at it with all your heart, as working for the Lord, not for men, [24]since you know that you will receive an inheritance from the Lord as a reward. It is the Lord Christ you are serving.
Colossians 3:22-24

My other bodyguard, Kirk Bentley, was in his late forties and the polar opposite of David in terms of temperament. He was also very funny and could make me laugh, but he was a much more reserved and introspective person in general. Kirk's temperament was a close match to my own, actually.

When I was transferred to the regional office after my training period at the various individual MWR facilities, Kirk was already working there as the area manager, responsible for nine sites around the Baghdad International Airport, including the Victory Base Complex. He took over the 'duties' of escorting me around the base and on various errands. The soldiers saw us together so often, they would often say, "Here comes Evelyn with her bodyguard!" In the middle of a war zone, surrounded by weaponry and armed men everywhere you turned, we always had a good laugh about that.

Kirk was a kind and gentle man, and we shared many wonderful talks about our lives and families. He was a good Christian man, and set a wonderful example for all with his calm, reassuring demeanor.

Whenever there was a conflict, he always seemed able, more than anyone else, to resolve the issue and settle things peacefully. In any workplace, there will be problems between co-workers on occasion, whether due to misunderstandings or the simple clash of personalities. This is especially true in a stressful environment like Iraq. Kirk was very good at listening to all sides and making everyone feel like their voice was heard in such matters. He had a real talent for peacemaking.

I also noticed Kirk took pains to learn bits and pieces of different languages so that he could better communicate with the disparate staff members. This was a contrast to the ill treatment some of the TCNs (third country nationals) sometimes received. The Americans such as myself did almost all of the clerical and supervisory work in Iraq, but the sheer magnitude of the undertaking forced hiring on a global scale. Since people have a tendency to trust and bond with those most familiar to themselves, some of my co-workers did not always treat the non-Americans as well as they should.

But Kirk was wonderful with these people. He always seemed to know a few words in their native tongue to break the ice or raise a smile. I think in these cases the effort one makes to learn about another's culture is really all it takes to generate goodwill, and Kirk always made the effort.

He was especially good with the Iraqis who worked on base. They were almost always friendly and polite, and I never failed to receive a nod and a smile when they passed. Kirk treated them with the utmost respect and courtesy and saw to it that everyone in his purview did the same.

Kirk had a very difficult job, and he not only did it very well, but remained well-liked by all who knew him. Which can be a very hard thing to accomplish sometimes.

I knew of only one misstep Kirk made his entire time in Iraq, and it is also a very good example of his unique social skills.

When he first got to Iraq, he was waiting around with some co-workers and soldiers at the 'grand opening' of a new PX on the Tallil Airbase, near the city of An Nasariyah, southeast of Baghdad. The PX was actually just a tent, but nevertheless, well over a hundred troops were lined up, looking forward to the promise of a certain kind of candy bar from the States, heretofore unavailable in Iraq. That may sound silly, but little things like that matter when people are forced to do without the comforts of home for long periods. But the PX couldn't officially 'open' until a two-star general showed up for a photo op.

After about a half hour in the hot sun, the general showed up, shook some hands, and had his picture taken. Afterwards, the PX was opened and the soldiers allowed inside.

Kirk, always concerned for the troops, actually told the general the men had been waiting in the hot sun for some time, and asked, politely, what had taken the general so long to arrive. Well, everyone got very quiet. It was one of those times when a little mistake could go terribly wrong, but Kirk, in that single moment, learned more about protocol than most people learn in a lifetime.

He quickly made a joking reference to those vaunted candy bars and the likelihood of keeping chocolate from melting in the desert heat, and one of the most powerful weapons known to man melted the general's icy stare.

Kirk's sense of humor.

The general laughed. And Kirk laughed. And the laughter spread to those around them, and a moment which could have seriously damaged Kirk's reputation immediately made it. And he never made a mistake like that again.

As I said, Kirk had a difficult job, which he did with style, humor, and grace. He was invaluable to me in my efforts to perform my own duties, and I hope that I succeeded in that regard, as well.

My bodyguards were as different as two men could be, but both Kirk and David each made my time in Iraq much easier with their presence in their own unique ways. I am proud to call them friends to this very day.

Ralph Waldo Emerson once said, "To know that even one life has breathed easier because you have lived, that is to have succeeded."

Both of these fine men are a resounding success, in my book, and I am truly blessed to know them.

19

OF ASTRONAUTS AND EVANGELISM

Community

¹²The body is a unit, though it is made up of many parts; and though all its parts are many, they form one body. So it is with Christ. ¹³For we were all baptized by one Spirit into one body— whether Jews or Greeks, slave or free—and we were all given the one Spirit to drink.
1 Corinthians 12:12-13

Not long after Bobby and I returned from our trip to the Holy land, President Kennedy was assassinated in Dallas.

Like all Americans, we were shocked and saddened at the loss of a President, especially one so young and in such a manner. After the contentious election of 1960, the ship of state seemed headed toward portentous seas, with momentous changes on the horizon.

After the Soviet Union successfully launched the Sputnik satellite into space in the late 50's, there was fear the United States had somehow fallen behind its cold war enemy, until Kennedy gave his famous speech in 1961 promising to put a man on the moon by the end of the decade.

Our nation was facing new challenges daily, and our leaders were constantly in my prayers. Times may change, but the one constant must be our faith as a God-fearing nation.

Things were somber on base, as would be expected. The military was on high alert, as the situation around the world seemed to become even more uncertain.

It was only the previous summer when Kennedy made his famous speech in Berlin, and barely a year since the tense days of the Cuban missile crisis.

And just three weeks prior, the president of South Vietnam had been assassinated and replaced in a coup which only increased the sense of danger in that divided country and the region as a whole.

To think that only four years earlier, I had been a high school senior back in Louisiana with no notion of the amazing things I would see and experience in such a short time.

The world was changing, and so was I.

Bobby was assigned to a military base in Hopewell, Virginia for the rest of his two year tour, which was scheduled to end in August. I was happily pregnant, my first born having survived that ocean crossing and due to arrive in July. The timing was fortuitous, as the military provided all health benefits and we knew the baby would receive the very best of care.

We lived off base, and I was able to stay home and prepare to be a mother while Bobby served his final months of duty.

We wanted our child to share our birthplace and also allow both of our families to participate in the experience, so I took a train from Richmond back to Shreveport in early June to rest and prepare for the birth. Bobby was to follow on emergency leave closer to the blessed event.

Well, he tried very hard, but Bobby missed the birth by a few hours. But the look on his face when he arrived and gazed into the eyes of his son made up for it. I had never seen him so happy.

We had been through so much in the few short years we had spent together, exciting times and trying times, seeing the world and sharing so many unique experiences, but in that one moment I truly felt everything had fallen into place for us. Our love of the Lord, our commitment to serve, and the love and support we gave each other had come full circle.

We were truly blessed. The next chapter in our lives had begun, and we were eager to begin our ministry.

Bobby had to return to Hopewell to be discharged, so I stayed in Shreveport while he traveled back and completed all the usual end-of-commitment processing. I missed Bobby and would have liked to have had him there with me, but a new baby has the tendency to focus your attention, so the time went fast and before I knew it, Bobby and I and baby Bren had settled in at my parents' house, where we would stay until we were able to find a place of our own.

Bobby had planned to finish his degree at the Bible college, but given the circumstances he decided to stay in Shreveport and complete his studies via correspondence course.

Shortly thereafter, Bobby heard of a small, southwestern church in need, so he applied and was accepted in early 1965 as the new pastor of the United Pentecostal Church of Grants, New Mexico. Happy and excited, we packed up our car and drove across Texas and most of New Mexico to our new home.

The car was a Chevrolet sedan this time, which was much more comfortable than our last road trip, but I must confess I missed the little Bug on occasion. Bobby had actually arranged it so that we were able to bring the Volkswagen to the States in the cargo hold of the troop ship (I may have heard it rolling around down there!), and was able to sell it once we arrived for even more than we paid for it. Bobby's ingenuity never ceased to amaze me.

Grants is a small town off the famed route 66 in western New Mexico, known at the time for its uranium mines. The area was as different from Shreveport as night and day. We were used to humidity and lush green vegetation, but Grants was, of course, in the dry desert surrounded by mountains.

Even so, we absolutely loved it. It was an adventure, and we were tremendously excited. Our first pastorate!

The church had a membership of about sixty, which is a fine size for a first time pastor, in my opinion. The people were exceedingly friendly and welcomed our little family with open arms. We immediately felt right at home.

I would teach the teen Sunday school class and play the piano, and Bobby would preach twice on Sunday and hold Bible study each Wednesday night.

We enjoyed taking time out during the week to explore, getting to know our surroundings and the people in the area. Everything was new and quite beautiful to us.

The congregation was mostly in their thirties and forties, which seemed ancient to me at the time. How one's perspective changes as you get older! There was, however, one single woman my age, Ida Montano (later Foster), with whom I bonded almost immediately. Many years later she would marry an Australian missionary while evangelizing in New Zealand, and I even spent one of my R and Rs with her, touring the outback. She is one of my closest and dearest friends to this day.

During my time in Grants, Ida would often come to the house in the evenings for dinner or just to talk and visit. It was nice to have someone my own age to converse with, especially a wonderful Christian like Ida.

Bobby and I had friends from school living in neighboring Colorado at the time, and who thought we would like their area. They told us about a small Pentecostal church in the town of Longmont, a bedroom community of Boulder, so we went for a visit.

It was a charming area, as was the church, which had been unused for nearly a decade. I could see the excitement in Bobby's eyes immediately. He had a restless nature, and was always looking for new opportunities to serve the Lord. Bobby saw in that vacant building, potential others might have missed. We prayed about it and felt the Lord's call to reopen the church.

Bobby went to visit the United Pentecostal Church Superintendent for the state of Colorado and other church officials, who were thrilled at the prospect of someone reopening the church, but there was no money in their budget to do so. If Bobby and I wanted to move to Longmont, we would be allowed to use the property but there would be no funds available for his salary.

For a young couple with a new baby, there were many things to consider, but as in every decision, we gave it up to the Lord.

After more prayer, we decided to continue in spite of the hardships. This was just the kind of challenge Bobby loved, and we trusted the Lord would help us find a way to make it all work out. Bobby had always been a real man of action, God's man, and I had faith in the talents with which the Lord had blessed him.

We soon moved to the nearby town of Loveland and began looking for work as we fixed up the structure to ready it for services. Obviously, having been vacant for ten years, it needed a lot of repairs and cleaning before a good coat of paint could be applied.

The building consisted of an adorable auditorium and two classrooms, as well as a parsonage attached at the rear. As soon as we could make it livable, we would be able to move into the back, which would be much more convenient and also very helpful financially. But our first priority was always the church itself, so we could begin holding services as soon as possible.

We both found jobs fairly quickly, so we worked during the week and cleaned and painted the church on weekends. Sometimes friends would help, but most days it was just the two of us, working long hours as baby Bren looked on.

Thinking back on that time, it sounds difficult, and it certainly was. But it was in service of the Lord, and we were completely content in our task. It was yet another example that happiness is being where God wants you to be. No matter the difficulty of the circumstances, that is always where true satisfaction lies. This is a message that's easy to miss, these days, and easy to forget in a society such as ours with all our creature comforts. In spite of all the distractions available, God is truly all you need.

Bobby found a job selling Pontiacs at a dealership in Denver. It was somewhat amusing when his customers discovered they were buying a car from a preacher, but I imagine, given the reputation car salesmen sometimes engender, a bit comforting, also.

I found work at Ball Brothers Research Corporation, first as a temp, and later full-time as a marketing administrator. Ball Brothers was founded back in 1880 with a loan from a minister to his nephews, who eventually developed their famous home canning jars which were once so ubiquitous before everything was store-bought. Ball State University in Muncie, Indiana was named for the family, who purchased some of the buildings on campus during its early years.

By the time I worked for them, the company had branched out into the aerospace industry, providing goods and services for NASA, including one-of-a-kind space instruments for such programs as the Orbiting Solar Observatory and the Saturn 5 moon rockets. I often interacted with scientists and engineers working on the Saturn 5 and Apollo space programs.

One of the interesting aspects of my job was giving guided tours of the facilities to some of the astronauts in the Apollo space program.

Unfortunately, I began working there not long after the terrible tragedy that befell Apollo 1, which caught fire on the launch pad and took the lives of Gus Grissom, Ed White, and Roger Chaffee, so my first days there were rather somber.

Still, their sacrifice only seemed to intensify the resolve of those working on the project to do their part to help America win the space race. Their deaths would not be in vain.

Sometime later I escorted the Apollo 8 crew of Jim Lovell, Bill Anders, and Frank Borman through testing areas, which were germ-free environments and required the use of special sterile clothing. This meant I actually 'suited up' with the astronauts.

Those same three men would later share a passage from the Bible with a worldwide television audience, broadcast from space. Millions of people all over the world listened as they took turns reading the first ten verses from the book of Genesis during their orbit of the moon on December 24, 1968, before wishing the entire world a Merry Christmas. It was a wonderful way to end such a tumultuous year in our history.

I later escorted Neil Armstrong, Buzz Aldrin, and Mike Collins through the same areas. They would eventually crew Apollo 11 and, of course, two of them would become the first human beings to walk on the surface of the moon. Buzz Aldrin even took communion while on the lunar surface, a fact which he only revealed years later.

God truly is everywhere, and travels with us in our hearts, no matter where we journey. And like the footsteps of those astronauts still outlined in the dust of the moon, His presence is unchanging.

Meanwhile, back on Earth, it took about two months before Bobby and I got the little church ready for Sunday service, and with word-of-mouth and a little help from some Pentecostals in the area who had attended the church as children, we held our first service. Attendance: Fifteen.

We did not worry, however.

Matthew 18:20 says, "For wherever two or more are gathered in my name, there I am in the midst of them."

Our first service in that tiny church meant as much to our Heavenly Father as the largest crowd in the biggest auditorium.

And just like those three astronauts so many thousands of miles above the earth, we worshipped God. And our voice was heard.

20

FALLEN WARRIORS

Death

⁵²In a flash, in the twinkling of an eye, at the last trumpet. For the trumpet will sound, the dead will be raised imperishable, and we will be changed. ⁵³For the perishable must clothe itself with the imperishable, and the mortal with immortality. ⁵⁴When the perishable has been clothed with the imperishable, and the mortal with immortality, then the saying that is written will come true: "Death has been swallowed up in victory."
1 Corinthians 15:52-54

The most difficult 'duty' I faced during my time in Iraq was attending the memorial services of fallen soldiers. It wasn't a duty which was required of me, but rather one which I felt called to perform.

I have never enjoyed funerals, but then again, who does? I have buried two husbands, and as a pastor's wife of many years, attended services for many more. It is something I have never grown accustomed to, and hope I never do.

But in my role as a preacher's wife, I was helping my husband minister to those in times of loss, and often, but not always, it was for the families of the elderly. There is something easier laying to rest those whose lives have been long and full, with the happiness of children and grandchildren as a large part of their time here on earth.

In Iraq, of course, it was much different. These are fine young people, our nation's best, who, in times of war, have offered to fight for the freedoms we hold dear as a nation. Many are young fathers, new husbands, and the imprint of their lives is far too brief. To be taken from their loved ones at such a time is unbearable to imagine. So much lost potential. So many fatherless children, and children not to be.

To watch the loss of so many fine young men in their prime takes a toll, and it moved me deeply, as it would anyone.

Before I went to Iraq I wondered how I would handle it, and asked for the Lord's strength. One of the reasons I decided to go in the first place was because I felt like I had something to offer in the way of service, and what greater service to God than to comfort His children in their time of need?

So I prayed constantly for the courage to do what He would have me do, regardless of what that was. As I described earlier, ever since my brush with death in that car accident so many years ago, I try to determine God's path for me each and every day, and achieve it as best I can.

I am an imperfect vessel, but I desire to be filled with the Holy Spirit at all times. Yes, I am confident in my relationship with the Lord, but I have fears and doubts just like anyone else, maybe more. When I have written of feeling His perfect peace and overcoming those fears, I give all the credit to God. He is the one through which all blessings flow. He is the one behind any and all accomplishment, He is the power driving whatever goals I achieve. And it is in His name I give thanks for allowing me the opportunity, and giving me the strength and courage to follow His will.

It is with this humility I confess I was most worried about the memorial services. I had imagined many times what they would be like. It was a long time since I was the wife of a soldier, but I knew enough about the military to have some idea. But my mind was filled with questions.

What would I say to a soldier who lost his brother? How could I possibly bring comfort to these frightened young men facing their mortality at such an early age? These things weighed heavily on my mind long before I landed in Iraq.

Whenever I am faced with such worries, I remind myself to give it all up to the Lord. This is the wonderful thing about God. He is always there, patiently waiting to listen to any problem and bear any burden, if only we have faith.

For the first four months I did not attend any memorial services, for a variety of reasons. My work schedule did not allow it at first, as my assignments were constantly shifting to different areas and I simply did not have the chance. But I knew the opportunity would come, and I continued to pray for God to allow me to provide comfort when it was needed.

The first one was much as I imagined it to be. The soldier's picture was placed in a frame on a table, his weapon and boots displayed on either side. He was a young man who had frequented the recreation center where I was working at the time, and I specifically remembered his friendly, courteous demeanor.

One of his company members found me and told me the service was to be held the next day, and asked if I would come. I said yes without hesitation, and prayed that night for God's strength and grace.

The next day, as I sat there looking at the picture of that fine young man and watching each soldier pass by to touch his boot, or his dog tags, or kneel and pray, my heart ached for those he'd left behind. These boys were trained to depend on each other and always look out for one another, and I know the loss of one so close frightened them deeply. I knew each man was thinking he could be next.

The services were mostly attended by soldiers, but sometimes there were other civilians like me. I prayed with any soldier who came to me and some who didn't. I mostly just tried to be available to anyone who needed a kind word or a friendly face.

The memorials would usually last about a half-hour. The chaplain would say a few words, usually reading the obituary, and then invite any of the soldiers in the unit to speak. Most would not, but anywhere from one to four would stand up and mention something the young man had said or done.

Some of the soldiers were quite eloquent, and others would stand for the longest time before saying just a few words, whatever they could get out. It was difficult for all, though you could see some put up better fronts than others.

When the soldiers were through, the commanding officer would speak, sometimes relating words from the family, or a particular remembrance of the deceased. Often, a general would also speak. It was always very sober and respectful, although on occasion a soldier might stand and relate something funny his brother-in-arms had said or done.

There might be a song, and to close the soldiers would then file past the altar, taking a moment before the boots and weapon and whatever medals the young man may have been awarded. Often the commanding officer would kneel and pray.

The services were held at various times during the day or evening, depending on the particular unit and their mission. Word would get around pretty quickly.

None were easy, but the last memorial service I went to was by far the hardest.

The soldiers in this particular unit were very familiar to me. They were almost all about nineteen or twenty years-old, and had come into the MWR facilities on many occasions.

Their captain approached me while I was eating breakfast at the DFAC. He informed me his unit had lost four men, and the service would be held that evening.

What shocked me was that four of them had been lost all at once, which is not necessarily unusual, but it wasn't that common, either. I personally knew three of the four, and several others in the unit. And two of those three had been to see me in my office.

The soldiers were not supposed to be in the administrative offices, but some of the soldiers sought me out, regardless, for prayer.

The company was being sent out on nightly missions in very dangerous areas, and the men were worried about something happening again like what killed their brothers.

The IEDs (improvised explosive devices) which had been responsible for the deaths of so many of our soldiers, were being improved and were actually piercing the under-armored vehicles from beneath, resulting in incidents like this and ever increasing casualties.

I had often attended services for soldiers I barely knew or not at all, but these faces were very familiar to me. My heart grieved for the boys I knew, the faces I had seen, the hands I had held in prayer. I had a feeling this particular service was going to be difficult to take.

At the end of the service, I did not have the strength to file past the boots of the slain men after their brothers. I just couldn't do it. I felt weak, almost sick to my stomach, and when I stood up to leave I had to grip the chair in front of me to steady myself.

I stood there a moment and watched as the soldiers walked by those boots, most of them crying, just trying to hold it together until they could exit out the side door and into the warm night.

I finally was able to leave through the front door, and saw that most of the company was either sitting or kneeling just outside, weeping into the sand.

They were physically and emotionally exhausted, and their suffering was visceral. They didn't want to go back out, but apparently had been assigned another mission that very night. Most of them seemed at the breaking point.

I knelt next to the nearest soldier and held him in my arms like a child as he wailed. I didn't understand why these boys had to be sent out again so soon after the tragedy they'd suffered. Often, after such an event, the unit would be given time off, but not this time.

I went from soldier to soldier, trying to find some words of comfort, hoping and praying I was saying the right thing as I sat in the dirt and listened to them cry. It was all I could do to remain calm and hold back my own tears as I prayed with these frightened young men.

They had lost four of their own in a single night because their vehicles were not properly armored, and the very next night, exhausted and scared, they were being asked to go right back out and do it again mere hours after the brief memorial.

I felt so deeply for them all, they might as well have been my own children, and I certainly could not have endured that evening without my faith in the Lord.

It took me hours that night to finally calm down. What can you say to a child with no life experience in that situation? How can you explain what has taken you a lifetime's experience to learn?

This all took place before what the American public came to know as "the surge," which was the additional troops sent to Iraq to help quell the horrible violence associated with the insurgency.

The memorial services were a constant reminder to me that our soldiers needed help in their missions. There simply were not enough of them to safely carry out the task with which they had been charged. I didn't understand why they were so short-handed, and I constantly prayed for God's wisdom to guide the decisions of our leaders in these matters.

I was so very grateful when the surge was implemented. I realize there were those who were against sending more soldiers to Iraq at the time, but I had no doubt it was the right decision. Being over there and seeing those brave soldiers going out night after night with nary a break, and then attending the memorial services of those who died, made it very clear to me that a surge was not only needed, but absolutely imperative.

Later events would, of course, prove that this was the correct strategy.

But at the time, it was just very difficult to realize what the soldiers had to deal with, and that last memorial service in particular really brought the issue home for me in a way that was both painful and illuminating.

I wanted so desperately to help those young men and yet I knew that I, too, was near my breaking point.

All I could do was pray that the Lord would bring them peace and try to remain calm for them.

Please God, help these young men.

Give them strength, Lord. Give them peace.

I was emotionally drained, and I never attended another memorial service during the short time I had left in Iraq.

I had finally reached my limit.

Give them strength, Lord.

Give them peace.

21
BACK TO THE BASICS

Priorities

[15]Then he said to them, "Watch out! Be on your guard against all kinds of greed; a man's life does not consist in the abundance of his possessions
Luke 12:15

Growing up, my parents taught me to save my money if there was something special I wanted to purchase. As I wrote earlier, my mother sewed most of my clothes when I was young, and because of her hard work I made sure to take very good care of them. This attitude carried over to all of my possessions, and because I paid for my own special things, I learned to be thrifty and to cherish the fruits of my labor.

As a girl, my father would pay me a dollar for every hour I practiced on the piano. I had other chores, too, and gradually earned the money to buy the things I wanted. And because I bought them with my own money, I learned to take extra care with my things so that I could enjoy them for years. It is a habit I continue to practice. Even now, I am not one who needs to buy new clothes each season, or to replace furnishings on a whim. These are the values instilled in me by my parents, and values I have passed on to my children and grandchildren.

Waste not, want not.

During our two years in Europe, I collected pieces of crystal, which I lovingly displayed in a beautiful French provincial china cabinet. Bobby and I were not wealthy, and our tastes were simple. There were many things we did without, as most young couples learn to do.

The crystal was really our only extravagance, and I enjoyed searching for new pieces to add to my collection whenever we traveled. I have always loved to shop, and whenever it was affordable, I purchased pieces to add to the collection. Some pieces were more inexpensive than others, but their beauty made them valuable to me, and I chose them with great care.

Whenever we had visitors, they always commented on the lovely display. I delighted in asking guests to point to any single piece or group which they found particularly intriguing so I could tell them the story of when and where they were purchased and what was happening in our lives at the time. Some of them I bought together, and some were single pieces, but they all had little stories behind them.

I had collected a total of seventy-two pieces while Bobby was stationed in France. I imagined some time in the distant future when Bobby and I would celebrate our fiftieth wedding anniversary, and we would trace our history through hundreds of pieces of beautiful, gleaming crystal. It was a romantic notion which Bobby happily indulged.

One day, I would tell him, we'll pass them on to our grandchildren, relating the unique story behind each piece as a way of telling them the story of our lives.

Before we left France, I carefully packed each piece, and was delighted when I lost not a single one during that rough ocean crossing. The crystal made the trip with us to Shreveport, and then on to New Mexico, with none the worse for wear.

They were my pride and joy, in terms of material possessions, and I continued to show them to my friends and tell the stories of their purchase. They were little souvenirs of our journey; reminders of where we'd been.

Once in New Mexico, Bobby and I purchased a trailer in which we would live, parked on church property. We set up our little home, moving in all our furniture, including, of course, my china cabinet with all my crystal treasures. Moving is always a chore, and when everything was unpacked I took particular care arranging them in the cabinet exactly how they had been before. I always knew we were 'home' when I had finished my crystal.

Shortly thereafter, Bobby decided the trailer was not quite plumb, and asked me to sit on the dining room floor with a level while he set the trailer right with a jack. I watched the bubble intently as Bobby slowly and carefully jacked up the trailer outside.

The floor ever so slowly rose on one side, the little bubble ever closer to the horizontal line across the window in the center of the level. I was almost ready to call out to Bobby that the bubble was dead center, when it happened.

The jack slipped, and the china cabinet tilted downward, throwing open the glass door and spilling dozens of my little treasures out onto the floor.

I was stunned.

Bobby rushed inside, only to find me on the floor, crying hysterically next to all that broken glass. I was inconsolable.

Poor Bobby. When he saw I was unhurt, he looked so relieved it only made me cry harder. Of course, I realized that when he heard the crash, he was desperately afraid the cabinet had fallen on me, which explained his initial reaction. But sometimes a girl just needs to have a good cry.

Bobby switched gears pretty quickly to attempt to deal with my hurt feelings, without much initial success I'm afraid. I was devastated. But Bobby was patient with me, and what he did next is indicative of his character and something which shows just how wise he was.

He handed me the phone and told me to call my mother.

Bobby and my mother had always gotten along very well. They were kindred spirits, and could spend hours talking together to the exclusion of anyone else in the room. At that particular moment, Bobby knew that she was probably the one person who would know exactly what to say to me.

As I recounted the tragedy of my forty-one broken pieces of crystal, she listened patiently to my story of loss, told through sobs and hitched breath.

When I finally finished, she said quietly, "What is truly important in this life?"

Well, I was almost as surprised as the moment when the crystal crashed to the floor in front of me. Her simple question cut through my emotion like a knife. I literally could not speak.

After a moment, she spoke again:

"Set your affection on things above, not on things on the earth. Colossians 3:2."

Whenever Mother quoted scripture, it was always heartfelt. She did not throw around the Word of God carelessly, but with precision and meaning. She sensed my distress, and even if it was misplaced, she knew it was real, and she took it seriously.

While I pondered that, she gently asked me about my priorities. She reminded me that my health, family, and service to God were most important in this life. All other things of the world would soon pass away.

I began to cry again, ashamed at the importance I had placed on my crystal 'treasures.' I knew my mother was right.

Soon enough, my tears turned to laughter. I'm sure Bobby was wondering what on earth was happening with his crazy wife, sitting in broken glass and crying till she laughed and laughing till she cried, but when I hung up the phone I gave him a big hug and told him everything was all right.

To this day I remember the calm voice and precious spirit of my mother, gently nudging me back to an understanding of what's really important in our lives.

I still enjoy buying nice things, and struggle as much as anyone to resist developing an unhealthy attachment to worldly goods. It's difficult, but that experience long ago helps me every day to understand my priorities and remember what is most important in the grand scheme of things.

I decided against adding to my collection of crystal. Somehow, it just didn't seem quite as important as it once did.

I still have the remaining thirty-one pieces, which serve as a constant reminder of the lesson I learned that day.

But I cherish the memory of those lost pieces every bit as much as the unbroken ones I see each day, because they taught me a great lesson.

"For where your treasure is, there your heart will be also." - Luke 12:34.

22
PLUGGING INTO POWER
Prayer

*[24] Therefore I tell you, whatever you ask for in prayer,
believe that you have received it, and it will be yours.
Mark 11:24*

I will never forget an incident which occurred in the office during my last year in Iraq. A young soldier in a terrible state rushed in. You'll remember some of the men had made a habit of stopping in to pray before their missions. This particular young man, like so many others, had been going out every night without a break, and he was absolutely petrified. He was beside himself with fear and anxiety. I had seen many young men during my time in Iraq who were fearful, but the look in this boy's eyes was a look I'll never forget. There was an intensity that was both visceral and unsettling.

We tried to calm him, but he was so panicked he seemed almost on the verge of a nervous breakdown. His mind was a battlefield, and the war raging inside was as fierce as any he faced with his battalion.

Shirley looked at me and I could see that she was wondering if one of us should call for a medic to help him.

As I've said before, the soldiers were not supposed to be in the administrative offices, and we certainly didn't want to cause him any trouble. The last thing this poor young man needed was anything to add to his distress.

Some officers were definitely more sympathetic to the challenges facing their young charges than others, and some soldiers were unwilling to seek help for psychological distress. Some of the men felt uncomfortable showing what they perceived as weakness to their superiors.

Shirley and I began to pray with him.

I felt the Holy Spirit enter the room, and we laid hands on that soldier as we prayed. I could tell that Shirley felt His presence, as well.

We began to pray louder, and our words merged as the Holy Spirit moved us.

"Father, we humbly ask You to bless this man and deliver him from harm. Please blanket him with Your shield of protection, that he might remain safe tonight, and every night. Thank you Lord. Your will be done. In Jesus' Holy name we pray, Amen."

I took hold of his hand, and looked straight into his eyes.

"You will be surrounded by the shield of God tonight. He will keep you safe."

With that he calmed down, gave us both a hug, and left us alone in the office.

Shirley and I went back to work, drained by the experience. So many soldiers we had prayed for, and each time it was an emotional experience. The Lord works in mysterious ways, and we cannot presume to know His will. All we can do is pray and leave the rest to Him. But I felt the Holy Spirit in the room that day, and I knew that young man would be all right.

Many times I would pray for a soldier, but never know his ultimate fate. He might be transferred and I would never hear from him again. Some soldiers with whom I interacted, playing chess, or in prayer, I later discovered had been killed or injured.

It was very difficult, constantly wondering how they were, these young men I saw every day. My heart ached for them. Oftentimes, as I lay in bed at night, listening to the sound of so many heavy trucks leaving the camp in convoys, I would pray myself to sleep, asking the Lord to keep them safe until the morning.

The next day, we got word that the soldier's convoy had been hit later that same night, and he had been hurt. We were not told the extent of his injuries.

His wife, who was ex-military and worked in MWR at another camp, was to be flown in to see him. I began the paperwork to permanently transfer her to our camp as Shirley and I prayed for his swift recovery and awaited news.

Shortly thereafter, who should walk through the door but the soldier himself! He had suffered nothing more serious than a concussion, and had already been cleared by the medics to return to duty.

"I just had to come by and thank you for praying with me yesterday," he said, and recounted the previous night's attack. The humvee in which he was riding was completely destroyed by an IED, but no one was killed! He told us the first thing that went through his mind in the chaos immediately following the explosion was our promise he would be protected by God's shield.

Moments before they were hit, he had felt compelled to move his weapon to his opposite side, which prevented much more serious injuries.

I believe the other soldiers in that humvee were protected because they were near that soldier, surrounded by the shield of God.

He was so different from the day before. I recognized the look in his eyes. It was a look I had often seen on my own face in the mirror after much prayer. It was the look of God's peace. He was going out again that very night, but the fear was gone from his eyes. He was a completely different person.

I thanked the Lord I had been there to pray for that soldier, and once again I was struck by the way God places us right where we need to be, if only we are open to His will and willing to receive His blessings.

By being there for that soldier in his time of need, God once again reminded me of my own mission and gave me a boost when I needed it most. I often reflected upon the fact that I could pray for these soldiers just as easily from my home in the states, but the experience and the personal contact would not have been possible were I not there in Iraq.

Just where He wanted me to be.

Lately I had been feeling like I could no longer 'take it' in Iraq. At that moment, God placed that soldier in my office. And that soldier, to whom I sought to provide comfort, ended up comforting me as well.

As I laid hands on him and felt the Holy Spirit move through me to ease the fear and trepidation in that young soldier, the Spirit also eased my own fears and trepidations.

The Holy Spirit had used us both.

God is so good!

Before he left our office that day, Shirley and I prayed with him once more. Once again, I felt the power of the Holy Spirit in the room.

We asked him to tell his entire squad that we were also praying for them whenever they went out, and the blood of our Savior Jesus Christ would be upon them, to keep them safe.

I never heard of any further casualties in his battalion, and I truly believe the Lord put him and his fellow soldiers under His protection.

Shirley and I had a wonderful praise session after he left, and marveled at God's power and grace. We had ourselves a time that day, and the incident helped us to maintain a spirit of prayer and fellowship the rest of the time we worked together in that office.

Long after I returned to the states, I looked back on that day as one of my very best in Iraq.

23

TREASURES OF THE HEART

Hope

³Praise be to the God and Father of our Lord Jesus Christ! In his great mercy he has given us new birth into a living hope through the resurrection of Jesus Christ from the dead, ⁴and into an inheritance that can never perish, spoil or fade—kept in heaven for you, ⁵who through faith are shielded by God's power until the coming of the salvation that is ready to be revealed in the last time. ⁶In this you greatly rejoice, though now for a little while you may have had to suffer grief in all kinds of trials. ⁷These have come so that your faith—of greater worth than gold, which perishes even though refined by fire—may be proved genuine and may result in praise, glory and honor when Jesus Christ is revealed
1 Peter 1:3-7

During our time in New Mexico, and later Colorado, Bobby and I worked tirelessly to grow the congregations of the tiny churches we served. Once we arrived in Longmont, Colorado, it was particularly difficult because the church had remained unused for so many years. We were literally starting from scratch, building the membership one person and one family at a time.

But we were not discouraged. Joshua 1:9 says, "Have I not commanded you? Be strong and of good courage; do not be afraid, nor be dismayed, for the Lord your God is with you wherever you go."

Joshua had been charged with leading two million people to conquer a strange land. Talk about a challenge! So God reminded him He was always

129

with him, to support Joshua in each task. And Joshua brought down the walls of Jericho. Every new job or assignment can be frightening, but with God in our lives it can be an adventure.

Bobby and I may not have been charged by God with conquering nations, but just like Joshua, He was there with us each and every day. The Lord is always with us in whatever difficult situations we may encounter. He will never abandon us, nor fail to help us. We must only place our trust in Him.

In a way, our church in Longmont was brand-new, and that made every congregant that much more precious. We rejoiced in the Lord whenever a new face wandered into the little auditorium.

Evangelizing for the Lord is truly the most rewarding task I have ever known. There is simply no experience to match seeing the joy in the eyes of a new believer who gives their life to Jesus, or the face of a strayed Christian who rediscovers the way of the Lord. It is a wonderful feeling.

The purpose of our lives together, all the moves, the jobs, the hard work; all of it was geared to share the message of salvation and sustenance so that others would also know God's perfect peace. It filled our hearts and nourished our souls, and something that awesome simply cannot be contained within. It was as natural as breathing in and out. The Lord filled us with the Spirit, and so we spread His word.

We cherished every opportunity to stop and share with whomever we met, even when our time together in Longmont was limited because of Bobby's traveling. There was no better way to spend our time than sharing the most important part of our lives with those hungry for the word of God.

All glory and praise be to Him when His message is shared and souls are won. We were grateful just to be able to do His will.

Bobby and I were both working full time during the week because the United Pentecostal Church, as I've related, did not have the funds at that time to support our efforts in Longmont. I was working at Ball Brothers, and Bobby was employed by the dealership in Denver. Eventually, Bobby took on even more outside responsibility in addition to his pastoral commitment. He was always a hard worker, with a tireless devotion to God and family.

The manager of the auto dealership where Bobby worked started a new business servicing sewing machines, and put Bobby in charge of all repairs in the eastern half of the state of Colorado. This meant he was traveling most of the week and ministering on the weekends, on top of his work in the community to spread the word of God and drum up support for our fledgling membership.

And of course, I was working during the week, caring for our toddler, and putting in many hours in support of our church, as well. I sometimes get a chuckle now when I read about modern women who wonder if it's possible to 'have it all,' as it's so commonly phrased. I suppose I 'had it all' during those years, but I was just doing what I had to do to survive, as was Bobby. I was blessed with a husband who shared my passion for the Lord's work, and a strong relationship with my Heavenly Father.

Bobby and I were happy, but it was still a taxing time. We missed spending time together during the week, and so it was a difficult adjustment when he took that second job. But we quickly learned to appreciate our time together even more. What a waste of energy it would have been to dwell on our time spent apart, instead of cherishing the hours we spent together.

Bobby and I had our problems, of course, like any couple. There were times we did not see things eye-to-eye. But because our love for each other was surpassed only by our love for the Lord, we had a strong, healthy marriage. When a relationship is steeped in faith, it is stronger than any conflict you will encounter. As in all things, we gave ourselves and our new family up to the Lord, and He provided us with inner peace and joy despite the hardships.

We were still young, and believe it or not, after a few years of marriage, we were still learning more about each other every day. Our love deepened as our faith grew, and the birth of our son was a blessed, transformational event in our lives. As hard as things were, it was a wonderful time for us.

The experience of spending so much time apart, relatively early in our marriage, probably helped prepare me in some small way, as much as anything could, for the loss of Bobby later on.

Not because I got used to being without him, far from it. I miss him even today, after all these years. But because of that experience, Bobby and I learned to make the most of our time together. We didn't waste energy on petty disagreements when our time together was so precious. We learned what was important in our relationship, and we focused our attention on each other. We got our priorities straight.

But I certainly miss him.

Rarely a day passes when he doesn't cross my mind. Sometimes it's fleeting and unexpected, like the flash of a firefly on a summer night.

And sometimes the memory lingers, and I allow myself to imagine the light touch of his hand against my cheek.

Often I wonder what he might think about a particular subject, or how he would react to something one of his sons said or did.

I don't feel sorry for myself, because I've had a wonderful life. I remarried, to a fine Christian man of whom I knew Bobby would approve, and have been inordinately blessed throughout my life.

But I do grieve for my grandsons, who will never bounce on Bobby's knee, or hear his booming laugh, or look into the soft, brown eyes of their grandfather as he tucks them in at night.

I take comfort in knowing they understand their Grandpa is with Jesus, and he's watching over them with pride in everything they do.

Those two years in Colorado gave me a very important gift, a lesson which has continued to grace my life. Like the broken crystal which taught me not to embrace possessions, the days Bobby and I spent apart taught us to make sure our time together was special and well-spent.

Time with your loved ones is so very precious; never, ever take it for granted.

Those days with Bobby are as vivid in my memory as if they'd happened yesterday, and I thank the Lord for allowing me to experience them, and to share them now.

These are my treasures.

My crystal.

My heart.

24

BLESSINGS FROM A FRIEND

Friendship

⁹ Two are better than one,
because they have a good return for their work:
¹⁰ If one falls down,
his friend can help him up.
But pity the man who falls
and has no one to help him up!
Ecclesiastes 4:9-10

Sharon Gillis is one of those treasured friends whose presence has made my own life immeasurably richer. From the time we met in the early 90s, she has had such a wonderful impact on my life in so many ways that I give thanks each and every day for her friendship. She is one of many awesome friends whom the Lord has used to bless my life.

After Bobby's death, I was remarried to a wonderful Christian man by the name of Bob Chriswell. Like Bobby, Bob was a preacher, and his flock was in Indiana, not all that far from where I had my car accident all those years ago.

I missed Louisiana, and Bob and I made frequent trips back to see family and friends. Sharon was friends with my younger brother, Verdell and his wife Galyn, and she was always around when I came to town. She loved the Lord, was close to my age, and had a vibrant, outgoing personality. We quickly became fast friends. I always thought it was a shame she never knew Bobby, as they were both so gregarious I know they would have gotten a real kick out of each other.

Sharon is the sister I never had.

In 1995, when my husband Bob was terminally ill, we moved back to Louisiana. Sharon was there for me during that difficult time. She is one of those friends you can always count on, and for months during that difficult time, she would drop everything and come running if I needed help with anything at all, even if it was just a shoulder to cry on. That experience deepened our friendship and she truly became my very best friend. I would trust her with my life, and I know she feels the same way.

There is something very comforting in having a friend like that, someone to whom you can say anything, without fear. Someone who will offer support, no matter what the nature of the problem, is a real treasure. Friends like that don't come along every day. Sharon is truly a gift from God in my life.

We are very different in temperament, but our personalities are complimentary and we've never shared a cross word in all the years I've know her. We also share many similar life experiences which helped forge the bonds of our friendship.

She has two beautiful grown daughters to match my two sons, and we each have three precious grandsons. Her youngest daughter married one of my cousins and the couple became good friends with my son Byron and his wife Stephanie. In so many instances, our lives have become intertwined in positive ways.

We both share a love of Christ and the desire to help those less fortunate. We worked together at ACS/Concera, which was the agency that coordinated long term care for the elderly. Her companionship in the workplace was also very precious to me. She helped me enormously in a difficult job, bringing joy and organization into my office.

I have written previously about a Christian's need for fellowship, and Sharon has provided much love and laughter in that regard.

Many times I have been amazed that the Lord has placed one of us right where He needed us to be to comfort the other.

Not long after Bob's death, Sharon lost her own husband and suffered the death of her mother in the same year. I know it was one of the toughest times of her life.

I was so grateful to be there for her during that time, and returned to her the wonderful, giving spirit she provided me during my difficult time.

"A friend loveth at all times, and a brother is born for adversity." - Proverbs 17:17.

I truly believe God brought us together to prop each other up in times of need, and to help each other find His path for our lives.

As I've mentioned, Sharon is also one of the reasons I found the courage to go to Iraq.

Sharon had been contemplating going to Iraq for some time, and during 2003, we had even spoken of signing up together. But when she left early the next year, I would not accompany her. I was, however, with her in spirit, and in absolute awe of her strength of purpose and steely resolve.

Sharon had never even been out of the United States, and here she was, literally preparing to enter a war zone on her first trip outside the borders of her homeland!

She was truly an inspiration.

Since I had not quite been ready to go at that time, Sharon left without me in early 2004. Her experiences there definitely helped paved the way for my decision to follow her later that year. I missed her terribly, but marveled at the phone calls and e-mails which described her experiences.

She was in Baghdad during the first attack on Fallujah, which was, of course, a very frightening time. But her missives were always filled with the spirit of the Lord, and she was not afraid. She seemed, to me, like Daniel in the lion's den, and her courage inspired my own.

She was there when the truck driver Thomas Hamill was taken, and rejoiced when he escaped.

Sharon felt her decision to go to Iraq had truly changed her life and deepened her faith. She felt renewed, and I could sense it every time we spoke. Her faith strengthened my own.

She also met many amazing people there. One of her co-workers was a vibrant young woman from Kosovo named Mirsade, whom everyone called Mercedes. This extraordinary young woman was supporting her entire family back home after the death of her father, and was a constant source of inspiration to Sharon, with her friendly disposition and strong work ethic. Sharon worked with her twelve hours a day, seven days a week, and Mercedes was one of many fine people who exemplified the very best results of U.S. efforts to foster goodwill and spread democracy to other countries and cultures. The foreign nationals who worked with U.S. personnel were on the front lines, and those very people are often the bridge to building relationships with other nations.

It did my heart good to hear how Sharon and Mercedes' friendship developed. Sometimes it's easy to forget that people all over the world want basically the same things as we do, and how much good can be achieved through personal contact and cooperation. Sharon's influence on Mercedes, and vice-versa, was one small step in the right direction.

I was beginning to feel more confident that not only could I find the strength and courage to follow my dear friend Sharon into the lion's den, but that I could, in some small way, make a difference myself.

As I continued to pray about my own decision, her e-mails and stories brought me closer to accepting God's will for my life in this most difficult decision. I have said many times that God's path was not always the one we expected, and many times He leads us to the most surprising places. But we must always strive to be where He wants us to be.

I know the Lord was working through Sharon when she wrote:

"I have taken so many things for granted all my life and it has been an awakening in my heart and mind just how precious our families, friends, and lives are. God has blessed me in so many ways it will take me the rest of my lifetime to thank Him. I pray every day that the remainder of my life will reflect what He has done for me…I am one very blessed girl and I give all the glory to God!"

Needless to say, then, as now, Sharon has inspired me in so many ways. I am so very grateful she allowed the Lord to use her during those months in such a way as to enable me to follow His path and to once more get to where He wanted me to be.

There is nothing on earth more valuable than a friend like Sharon.

She has truly been a blessing in my life.

25

RESTLESS SERVANTS

Revivial

17 "'In the last days, God says, I will pour out my Spirit on all people.
Your sons and daughters will prophesy, your young men will see visions,
your old men will dream dreams.
18 Even on my servants, both men and women,
I will pour out my Spirit in those days, and they will prophesy.
19 I will show wonders in the heaven above
and signs on the earth below, blood and fire and billows of smoke.
20 The sun will be turned to darkness and the moon to blood
before the coming of the great and glorious day of the Lord.
21 And everyone who calls on the name of the Lord will be saved.'

After spending two years in New Mexico, and another two years in Colorado, Bobby decided he needed to make a change. The tiny church in Longmont simply wasn't growing as fast as he wanted.

My husband was a servant of God, but he was a restless servant. He was still a young man, not yet thirty, and like all men, preachers and laymen alike, sometimes it takes awhile before they settle into themselves.

So we talked about it, as we did all things. We never had problems with communication in our marriage. Even in our early years together in France, though I may have been a little overmatched at times in terms of will, Bobby was always so solicitous that I would have my say even if it didn't always occur to me to present it.

Bobby was such an empathetic person that he drew out my true feelings even when I preferred to keep them inside. That was one of the qualities which made him a wonderful preacher, along with his keen insight into human nature.

But by this time I was more of a match to his strong personality. I grew into him, and I know that he adapted to me, also. Our personalities, though quite dissimilar initially, drifted ever so slightly into a comfortable orbit which we both could navigate. I think when you find your soul mate, you naturally begin to compliment each other's personalities in positive ways. We brought out the best in each other.

I could feel his anguish. I knew above all he wanted to serve God and love his family, and he had done both faithfully for eight years. But he wanted to accomplish more. He felt called to do more. He ached to serve God.

And his need was my own.

Bobby desired to do great things for the Lord, and he felt that might not happen as quickly as he wanted it to in Colorado. I reminded him that he had already accomplished much in service of the tiny congregations, but I understood what he meant. Bobby was still searching for his place in the world. He was still a young pastor finding his way, looking for the best way to serve God. And he felt the Lord calling him in a different direction.

After much discussion and prayer, we decided to leave our little church in Longmont and return home. We packed up our things and went back to Louisiana to prepare for the next phase of our lives.

It was good to be home. In spite of all our blessings, I had felt unsettled the last several years. It seemed just as we were putting down roots in one place, we were called to the next. But God's path is not always the easy path, and as long as we were where the Lord wanted us to be, I was satisfied.

But the Lord had much more traveling in store for our little family.

The next three years were to be the most tumultuous, yet rewarding years of our young lives.

We were called to the revival circuit.

There was a real need for revival all across the country. The rough decade of the 60s, with the assassinations, riots, and political turmoil, was coming to a close. The Vietnam War was being fought in full force. More and more young people were turning to drugs and promiscuity. Time magazine even asked on its cover, much to our horror, "Is God Dead?" It was a time when the nation seemed to cry out for the Word of God.

So our little family decided to hit the road.

But before we did, Bobby felt compelled to prepare himself in a way he never had before.

Bobby entered the wilderness to commune with God.

My father had a small trailer out in the woods which was used as a deer blind during hunting season. It was off season, so Bobby decided to put it to good use. He went out there to fast and pray and meditate for a month to prepare for our evangelism.

Bobby's mother dropped him off with a load of books, jugs of water, and little else. He asked that no one visit until the month was up.

Naturally, I was concerned, as was his mother, who, in spite of his entreaties, drove out once a week to leave fresh jugs of water on the step outside the trailer. She never saw nor spoke to Bobby the entire month, but found the empty jugs out front each time she returned.

Naturally, by the end of the month I was fit to be tied. I missed him terribly, and was of course very eager to see him after our time apart.

When I saw him, I was stunned. Of course he was bearded and shaggy, but there was something else about him which had changed. It was something in his eyes. He looked intensely peaceful, if that contradiction makes any sense at all. He had the look of a man who has seen the face of God and now must share the experience with the world. There was a new confidence in him, and I believe he had truly settled into himself and been touched by the hand of God.

I cannot begin to imagine the strength and resolve necessary to sustain such an endeavor, except that God was with him. Today I find it difficult to go a single day without eating, and yet Bobby was out there in the woods for an entire month without a single meal.

This was but the first of many miracles I was to witness in the coming year.

We began to travel all around the United States, up and down the eastern seaboard, and as far west as Montana.

The United Pentecostal Church sponsored us in small churches all over the country, most of whom could not afford to provide us with much more than a few groceries and a spare bedroom in their homes. Sometimes we even slept in an empty Sunday School classroom. Whatever they offered, we accepted and made the best of it.

Ironically, many were churches not unlike the two in New Mexico and Colorado. Bobby had prayed for bigger tasks and the Lord had answered him. He called Bobby into the wilderness and released him into the tents of civilization.

I noticed immediately a change in how Bobby preached. He was always passionate in the pulpit, but he was different now. He preached as if every word was on fire.

It sounds almost like a cliché, but there was electricity in the air when he sermonized. It was palpable and exciting, and many people accepted the invitation to invite Christ into their lives at the end of each service, which became progressively larger throughout the week as word spread in the community.

I was so proud of Bobby, and his passion inspired me, also. I felt closer to God each and every service, and as our faith deepened, so did our bond. We were maturing as Christians and as partners, and our love for each other and our son knew no bounds.

Even little Bren was part of the service. I would play the piano or organ if they had one, or sometimes the accordion, and sing a song or two before the sermon. Usually Bren would join me for one song with his tambourine. He was so adorable at four years-old, and he loved to join in with his mother before watching his daddy preach.

One night, near the end of the service, Bobby called for those who wanted to pray with him to come down the aisle. An older man was led to Bobby by his daughter. He was blind. Bobby took the man's hands in his own, and began to pray.

I could see them both start to sway gently as Bobby whispered into the man's ear. The blind man was nodding and crying.

Bobby began to speak faster and with more intensity, and the older man hugged him tightly.

Suddenly they stopped moving and the entire crowd grew quiet.

Bobby released the man from his arms, and looked into his eyes.

And the man looked back.

He could see.

The crowd gasped as the old man began to run to others in the congregation and grab their faces in his hands, looking into their eyes, laughing until he cried.

Several of his relatives came forward to verify he had indeed been blind, and needless to say, the next service was twice as large.

Word spread throughout the community, and churches began to call and request Bobby come to their town for revivals. It was a very exciting time, and after a year of the smaller churches which had been sponsored by the UPC, we began to evangelize at larger churches which were able to pay for our expenses from offerings.

We spent many months traveling to these churches and preaching to ever larger crowds, and I saw more people healed.

But even more important, many people during our three years of revivals publicly invited Jesus Christ into their hearts as Lord and Savior, and were baptized in the Holy Spirit as prescribed in the book of Acts. This was the most rewarding thing of all. This was what Bobby had prayed for out in the woods. This was what we had dedicated our lives to when we were first married. This was God's plan for our lives.

As I've written, it's an amazing experience to see the effect of Jesus in the face of a new believer. You are literally watching their rebirth in Christ, and it is thrilling to see.

We were so very grateful to God for allowing us to witness so many lives given up to the Lord.

All of the glory goes to God for the things we witnessed. He is the potter, His servants the potter's clay.

After two years in France, two years in the west, and three years of revivals, we were both ready to go home. Bren was about to start school, so we returned once more to Louisiana, and unpacked our things for the first time in a very long time.

It seemed as if we had been gone for a lifetime, but we were together, and doing the Lord's work. We couldn't have asked for anything else.

We were certainly grateful to be home and beginning a new chapter in our evangelism, but the services during those years were some of the most memorable of my life.

P.V. & Hope Webb (my parents) - 1953

Jim Plunk, Evelyn & Bobby - Ephesus 1963

Bren, Bobby & Evelyn Dykes - 1970

Bren, Byron, Evelyn & Bobby Dykes - Paris, France 1975

Evelyn, Bob Chriswell, 1982

Bob Chriswell's grandchildren: Melanie Chriswell's children - Lauren, Andrea, Nathaniel, Christopher, and Cindy's child - Jessica -2010

Evelyn with Arabs - February '05

Bunker Toilet - Logbase Seitz

David, Shirley on helicopter

Evelyn at judges bench of Saddam's first hearing

Evelyn attempting to hold weapon

Evelyn in a Stryker Vehicle Oct 24 '06

Evelyn with Iraqi soldiers

Evelyn, Reggie Myre, Byron & Sharon - In line for Christmas dinner at Camp Striker 2004

Evelyn in office during sand storm August 8, '05

Evelyn, Sharon - bullet ridden truck

Haifa votes in Referendum - October 15, 2005

Kirk Bentley, Byron Dykes

Reenlistment at Al Faw Palace, Camp Victory, Baghdad

Sandstorm in Al Asad - April 2005

Living area after rocket attack in 2005

Shopping in Camp Victory, Iraq

Sharon, Evelyn with British soldiers posing for 2006 Christmas pictures

My grandsons - Bryton, Gevin, & Seth, who called me Baghdad Grambo

Some pictures can be seen in color at:
www.baghdadgrambo.com

26
KINDRED SPIRITS IN IRAQ
Church

19 Consequently, you are no longer foreigners and aliens, but fellow citizens with God's people and members of God's household, 20 built on the foundation of the apostles and prophets, with Christ Jesus himself as the chief cornerstone. 21 In him the whole building is joined together and rises to become a holy temple in the Lord. 22 And in him you too are being built together to become a dwelling in which God lives by his Spirit.
Ephesians 2:19-22

As I've said, I tried to attend as many chapel services as I possibly could while serving in Iraq, but working fourteen and fifteen hour days, seven days a week made things a little difficult at times.

Most of the time, I was able to get away from the office to attend Sunday evening services. The chaplains would usually rotate in for six months at a time, and I always looked forward to meeting the new preachers. Sunday night was the highlight of my week, and sitting down to hear a sermon was like putting my feet in a warm bath after standing all day.

I enjoyed attending with Shirley, and Kirk after she left, but there were many times when I went by myself. It was always such a dichotomous picture to see the soldiers praising the Lord with weapons at their feet. They were required to carry their weapons wherever they went, just as I described in the Christmas service, but it never failed to garner my attention.

It was always very moving to see these young men, who were prepared to make the ultimate sacrifice, so serious in their desire to worship. They were under such stress each and every day, and yet they came to these services during their time off to join with others in praise of their Creator.

These highly trained soldiers, who daily performed duties which most of us couldn't imagine, arrived at the tiny chapels scattered around base with more on their minds than war and the killing which is, unfortunately, a necessary and all too common part of their lives. Their interest in spiritual things was something I found very impressive.

I admired those men more than I can say.

The Sunday night services were called the "contemporary" services. More traditional services were held on Sunday mornings, and every faith you could imagine was represented. The military is very careful and sincere in its desire to provide whatever spiritual guidance each and every soldier requires.

Once when I invited one of my co-workers to a Pentecostal service, he told me he was afraid he'd see what he called "satellite" Christians. I had never heard this term, and asked him what it meant. He said satellite Christians were the ones he'd seen on TV with their arms waving in the air, as if their hands were antennas searching for the best possible signal from the Almighty.

Well, I had to laugh at that. I guess some Baptists are a little less demonstrative than Pentecostals. But we all receive our 'signals' from the same place.

There were sometimes chaplains of multiple faiths and branches of the military in a single service, and they each might even take a small part of the service to speak.

On Friday evenings, there was a special service, during which the chaplains would gather on a rooftop overlooking Baghdad, and pray for the city and its residents. That is one aspect of the war which is not widely known in the civilian world, and undoubtedly unexpected, but I think it shows the humanity and good intentions of our brave men and women over there.

I was never able to attend these particular services because of my work schedule, but just knowing those soldiers were up there made me feel very warm inside. On Friday evenings I would often glance outside and say a prayer of thanksgiving for those whose rooftop compassion shone so brightly through the smoke-filled skies of war, and asked the Lord to bless their hearts and give them strength.

Communion was offered monthly, and I always looked forward to partaking of the Lord's Supper with the soldiers, who were preparing their hearts and spirits for the dangers they faced outside the wire.

I visited as many different chapels as I was able. It was a little like the DFACs. I enjoyed the variety and was always looking for new experiences. Many of them were very rough, especially in the beginning of the war when just about everything was in tents.

Most of the TCNs (third country nationals) had their own special chapels, often in whatever space they could find near where they lived. The Filipinos, who were civilian workers, had a very tiny space set aside near their sleeping quarters, as did the Ugandans, who were all soldiers.

I greatly enjoyed the services I was able to attend held by the Ugandans, who were very sweet people. Their services were very vocal and joyous, much like many African-American services in the United States. I suppose they, too, were 'satellite' Christians.

There was usually music and singing in all the services, and often soldiers formed 'praise teams,' who would give spiritual reports on the week past, and assign smaller groups of about six to sing or play instruments if they were available.

Tigerland had its own baptismal tank, yet others simply had a washtub or even a plastic container to perform baptisms as the need arose. Others would utilize swimming pools when possible. Normally baptisms were scheduled about every six months at the chapel I usually attended.

I often thought back to the very first followers of Christ, who met in caves and other such places to escape persecution after the death and resurrection of Jesus.

Those early Christians were determined to worship no matter what the cost, and now I saw some of that same passion for the Lord two thousand years later near where it all began.

Just like the Ugandans, who are not really so different from us, so too were those initial followers of Christ similar in their beliefs.

God is unchanging, and His will everlasting. As Christians, it is so very important to remember who we serve. And why.

There is much more we share than what sets apart all those who love the Lord.

27
READY TO "GO!"

Evangelism

*He said to them, "Go into all the world and preach
the good news to all creation
Mark 16:15*

During the three years we spent traveling around the country and holding revivals, Bobby and I were occasionally able to come back to Shreveport for a week or two and visit with our families.

On one of our visits home in 1971, my mother was very ill. Her multiple sclerosis had progressively worsened over the last several years, and the emphysema had begun taking a very serious toll on her health, as well. It had become very difficult for her to breathe, and she was often wracked with fits of coughing and choking. Coupled with the general weakness and fatigue which comes with the muscular degeneration of MS, her doctor advised us that she would likely not live much longer than another year. This was another factor in our decision to come home to stay. I wanted to be there for my mother during her last days.

So Bobby, Bren, and I returned to Shreveport and settled into our life at home.

We rented a little house near my parents so I could help out with mother, and Bobby took a position as youth minister at the First United Pentecostal Church of Shreveport, where I directed the choir and orchestra. Bobby was also asked to preach at other churches in the surrounding areas, as many had heard of him through our years of revivals, and he readily agreed. We began building our life in Louisiana.

Almost immediately upon our return, I became pregnant with my second son, Byron. We were completely surprised by this blessed event. My first pregnancy had been very difficult, (even aside from that tumultuous ocean crossing at three months) and I fully expected Bren to be my only child. But any worries I had about another strenuous delivery were unfounded, and it was a much easier pregnancy from beginning to end. I joked with Bobby that had my first been that easy, we would likely have had several more children.

I gave birth to Byron exactly seven years to the day after Bren was born - July 7, 1971. So my sons share the same birthday.

Byron would later grow up to marry Stephanie, whose birthday was also the seventh day of the seventh month, which pleased me to no end. The number seven has very special significance in the Bible, and for years we celebrated all three birthdays every July 7th.

The number seven is symbolic of God's perfection. It appears many, many times in both the Old and New Testaments.

After creating the world and everything in it, God rested on the seventh day, a sign of perfection and completion. Noah was warned by God of the flood seven days before it started raining.

Jacob worked for seven years to earn the hand of Rachel in marriage, only to be tricked by Rachel's father, and so then agreed to work another seven years, so great was his love for her.

Jacob's son, Joseph, correctly interpreted the dreams of the Pharaoh that Egypt would see seven years of plenty, followed by seven years of famine.

In the New Testament, Jesus fed thousands with seven loaves and fishes, cast out seven evil spirits from Mary Magdalene, and taught that we must forgive others "seventy times seven," which means, of course, that there are no limits to the forgiveness we must offer our brothers and sisters.

Infinite forgiveness. What a beautiful message.

In the book of Revelation, there are seven churches, seven archangels, seven seals, and many more symbols and multiples of sevens.

Adam to Jesus spanned seventy-seven generations.

And, of course, we are all instructed to remember and keep as Holy, the seventh day, to rest as our Lord did, honoring God and all He created.

I always enjoyed our connection of 'sevens' and loved to recount the many Bible stories which conveyed that symbol of God's perfect love.

Many things have changed in my life and my family, but I use the story of sevens even today to teach my three young grandsons important lessons from the Bible. They are wonderful boys, as spiritual as they are precocious.

In the spring of 1972, Bobby began expressing his desire that we return to France as missionaries. Actually, he had wanted to go back practically from the time we left after his two year stint in the army. I was not so keen on the idea at the time, however, and we both agreed to answer God's call for service in the United States.

But it was always there in the back of Bobby's mind. There was something about the country that drew him in, and while he respected my feelings, Bobby never made his own a secret.

But I always resisted. I enjoyed our time there but was just not receptive to the idea of going back, and Bobby never pushed the idea. He would simply remind me every now and then, sometimes in small, subtle ways, and sometimes simply and directly.

We would discuss it on occasion, but all it would take was a shake of my head and Bobby would drop the subject. He knew when I just didn't want to talk about it, and we developed the shorthand all married couples acquire. He wouldn't dream of forcing the issue, and I respected his need to remind me from time to time of his desire to return one day.

As you can imagine, our lives were quite full as soon as we came back. We were settling in, I was pregnant and helping take care of my mother, Bren started school, and both Bobby and I were adjusting to our new duties at the church. And then came Byron, our second, beautiful son. We really had a wonderful life.

Hectic, but wonderful.

Bren doted on his new baby brother, who was born on his birthday and was enamored with the story of the sevens.

I'll never forget how, about two weeks after we brought his baby brother home, I explained to him that he and his brother would share the same birthday always.

He looked up at me, wide-eyed, and back down to the tiny baby in his arms. After a moment, he held little Byron up to me, and said in a very solemn voice, "Can we give him back, now?"

I guess the idea of sharing isn't always an attractive concept to a seven year-old. But fortunately, he soon got used to the idea of his little brother, and grew very protective of him after a while.

My grandsons today remind me so very much of my children, and I get such joy in seeing them at the same age as their fathers, even as I watch my sons raise them. They all bring me such happiness, and I see the same little personality quirks I saw in their fathers long ago, now with new eyes and a fresh perspective. When you are a parent, especially at a young age, there are so many things which seem to pass in an instant. If you're lucky enough to have grandchildren, it's almost as if you get another bite at the apple, and you can slow down and enjoy everything a second time.

Almost forty years later, during one of my R and Rs, my three grandsons announced they had a surprise for me and retired to a bedroom, imploring me not to come in until they were ready.

When they finally summoned me, I found my older son Bren's boys, Seth and Gevin, ages ten and seven, holding guitars, while Byron's five year-old son Bryton stood at his keyboard with a microphone. They were all in their underwear, and proclaimed themselves the 'Naked Cousins Band,' after the children's television show, and began to sing and play to my laughter and amazement. I wish Bobby could have enjoyed that moment with me.

But I digress. Grandchildren will cause you to do that.

In the spring of 1972, Bobby began once more to remind me of his desire to return to France. I was still not interested, but Bobby didn't pressure me. He was just sowing seeds, you might say.

That fall Bobby and I attended the United Pentecostal Church Conference in Houston, an annual meeting during which church members from all over the country gathered together to praise the Lord, plan for the coming year, and welcome missionaries from all over the world. There are training sessions and meetings during the day, and services each evening. It is always a wonderful time to meet new friends and spend time with old friends in loving Christian fellowship.

The UPC missionaries are sent out for four years, after which they may return to the States for a year to raise funds and gather pledges of support for the following four.

Many missionaries would speak at the services and report on the upcoming needs of the areas which they served, and the testimonies are truly inspiring.

There was also a call for missionaries to travel to countries which were not yet being served.

One evening, the great Pentecostal preacher James Kilgore gave the message. There must have been ten thousand people in the auditorium on that warm, humid night. I remember there was such a powerful feeling of compassion which swept through the crowd that night as thousands got down on their knees and prayed for those who didn't yet know Jesus. And as we were praying, I felt the presence of the Holy Spirit, who told me, "Now is the time."

And I knew in an instant that the Lord was calling me to go back to France to serve Him as a missionary, just as Bobby had wanted all those years.

I turned to my husband, but did not speak. He felt my eyes and opened his own.

"I'm ready to go," I said, but I didn't really need to speak at all. He could see it in my eyes.

He nodded and took my hand, and we bowed our heads together and prayed for the Lord's strength and guidance as we embarked on yet another unexpected path. (at least for me!)

Somehow I think Bobby may have known all along.

We went back to Shreveport inspired in our next calling, but I was worried about mother. I could not possibly leave the country when she was ill. As soon as we got home I went over to see her.

Before I could even speak, she motioned me over next to her bed. She had been having trouble breathing and her voice was often short and raspy, but she took my hand in hers and spoke very clearly, "I want you to go."

She and Bobby had always had a very special relationship, and she was well aware from our talks that he had always wanted to go back into mission work.

As soon as I walked in that door she could see it in my eyes. She knew Bobby and I had attended the conference, and I suppose my excitement over the mission and my concern for her could be read all over my face. She saw that, and she didn't want me to worry. She wanted me to be wherever the Lord wanted me.

At that moment I was so filled with love for her, and so very grateful to God I had been there with her during those past months.

Which was, of course, right where He wanted me to be.

And when my mother passed barely two months later, I knew she was going right where He wanted her to be, too.

And I knew she was ready.

28

AMAZING GRACE

Suffering

[36] Some faced jeers and flogging, while still others were chained and put in prison. [37] They were stoned; they were sawed in two; they were put to death by the sword. They went about in sheepskins and goatskins, destitute, persecuted and mistreated— [38] the world was not worthy of them. They wandered in deserts and mountains, and in caves and holes in the ground. [39] These were all commended for their faith, yet none of them received what had been promised. [40] God had planned something better for us so that only together with us would they be made perfect.
Hebrews 11:36-40

I have already mentioned that I love to shop, and my time in Iraq certainly did nothing to change that. I think most women like to examine things, comparing prices and colors and whatnot. It's as much a social activity as a commercial one. I've spent many a long afternoon shopping with a girlfriend and returning home with a little more than tired feet and a memory of wonderful conversation. Within the camp, there were many small vendors who were allowed to sell their wares in a bazaar-like fashion, with stalls and trailers lined up like games on a midway. I often enjoyed walking through the area with Sharon on a lunch break, looking over the knick-knacks, rugs, and various other crafts for sale.

The shopkeepers were mostly Iraqis, some of whom would walk as many as fifteen miles each day to come to the camp for the opportunity to work their little store for twelve hours before walking home again, seven days a week. The city at that time was still quite dangerous, and those Iraqis who worked in the camp tried to keep their destination a secret, lest they be targeted by insurgents for consorting with Americans.

There was one Iraqi shopkeeper in particular with whom I became quite cordial. She was a woman in her thirties, who ran the store with her husband. They were both nice, hard-working people, always eager with a smile and a friendly word. They were never disappointed if I didn't buy anything, and I looked forward to seeing them whenever I was able to cruise the shops. She showed me pictures of her children, two adorable young boys whose future she and her husband were working so hard to secure. A war turns the economy of a large city like Baghdad upside down, and working on base offered a steady means of support for many whose livelihoods had been, at least temporarily, disrupted. And of course, the insurgency not only prolonged the disruption, but made such alternative work highly dangerous. I admired this couple who were doing the best they could for their family under such difficult circumstances. One day when I went to their trailer, it was still padlocked from the night before. I thought perhaps one or the other was ill, and decided to check back as soon as I was able. I hoped for the best, but in a situation like that you never take anything for granted. I said a little prayer that night that I would see them the next time I returned.

But the trailer was still padlocked the next day, and the next week. Two weeks went by, and I asked some of the other shopkeepers, but no one knew why their little store was still shuttered. Two months went by before I found out what had happened. Insurgents had killed her husband just outside the Castle gate on his way into the camp the morning of that first day I found their trailer locked on my lunch hour.

I can't tell you how saddened I was by this news. I thought of those two young boys in the pictures she had shown me, who would now grow up without their father as would so many other children in this country.

I was not much older than this Iraqi woman when Bobby was killed unexpectedly, also leaving me a widow with two young sons. The similarities of our lives struck me, and I wondered if I would ever see her again. I wondered if I could possibly convey to her my feelings for her loss. I felt a real kinship with this woman, and it was yet another of the many reminders of our common humanity. These people, in so many ways, are very much like us. In spite of our differences, there is much more that binds us together as God's children. Most Iraqis just want to live in peace and freedom and find a way to provide a better life for their children.

The insurgents are different. They are a clear example of the dark forces which exist in the world today, and why it's so important to persevere in our fight against them.

How can people be so evil to one another? Did those who killed this man give a second thought to their own wives, their own sons and daughters, to how would they feel if their own families were destroyed, never to be whole again?

Ultimately, there was nothing I could do but turn to God. As always, I found comfort in His word and strength in the knowledge that He was watching over the shopkeeper and her boys just as He had watched over me and mine after Bobby's death.

So I prayed. I prayed not only for that family, but I prayed for myself. I asked the Lord to allow me to love not only the shopkeeper and her sons, but those who had killed her husband. I asked for the courage to forgive those men who had so senselessly taken that man's life. Infinite forgiveness. What a difficult message. Eventually, she came back and emptied out the little trailer, and another shopkeeper took over her space.

There were more deaths after that. Many more Iraqis who worked in the camps were targeted, and eventually so many were killed that there were only four or five shopkeepers arriving each day. Everyone else simply stopped coming in to work, including many of the Iraqis who worked in other capacities. One incident in particular stands out in my mind. A group of vehicles outside the gate was hit and twenty Iraqi workers were killed all at once. It was discouraging to see so many decent, hard working people continue to lose their lives, and eventually the CPA created an Iraqi dormitory within the camp so the workers could live on base. There was really no other option at that point, and I was grateful that accommodation had been made. As depressing as things could be, the Lord continued to bless me with reminders of His love and guidance.

Not long after the rocket hit those vehicles outside the gate, an Iraqi major approached me in the DFAC. We had developed a cordial relationship from the many times our paths had crossed. He spoke English fairly well, and we would exchange pleasantries whenever we saw each other, normally at mealtimes.

But this time he had tears in his eyes.

He said, "When you return home, please tell your American friends 'thank you' for allowing you to come to Iraq to help us." And he took my hand, which was unusual for him, and squeezed it in his briefly before striding out the door.

I am not sure what moved him to speak those words that day, but I was very touched by this, and it is one of the many reasons I have written this book.

It is so important for Americans to know how much we are appreciated for what we've done over there. There have been mistakes, but they are far outweighed by our accomplishments.

I also became friends with a young Iraqi interpreter. She was a 28 year-old Sunni, a college graduate with whom I shared many meals. She was a very sweet young woman who lived on base.

One day she seemed upset, and so I asked her what was bothering her. She told me that it had been weeks since she had seen or heard from her family in the city. She didn't know whether they were too intimidated to contact her or had been driven out of their home, as many had been throughout Baghdad. The more ominous possibilities remained unspoken between us, but we both understood.

I added her and her family to my prayers that night.

There were so many people I met while in Iraq, so many good people who made me appreciate even more our mission there, and my tiny contribution to it. I was thankful to God for allowing me to be there in His infinite wisdom, but it could be very difficult in times like that. God's will is not always easy, but it is always attainable if only we trust in the Lord. We are all God's children, and all are worthy of His amazing grace. There is nothing that would please Him more than for all His children to love each other. It is easy to pray for those good people. But God commands us also to pray for those who would do us harm.

> *"But I tell you who hear me: Love your enemies, do good to those who hate you, bless those who curse you, pray for those who mistreat you." – Luke 6:27-28*

I swallowed hard and continued to pray not only for those good people around me, my co-workers and our brave soldiers, but also those who would do terrible things to them if given the chance.

This is one of the hardest things the Lord calls upon us to do, and yet it's also one of the most important. What a different world it would be if only we could all love one another as He would have us do.

29
NEW HEART, NEW DIRECTION
Change

26 I will give you a new heart and put a new spirit in you; I will remove from you your heart of stone and give you a heart of flesh. 27 And I will put my Spirit in you and move you to follow my decrees and be careful to keep my laws
Ezekiel 36:26-27

My father was devastated after my mother's death. And was none too pleased to hear that Bobby and I had applied for mission status to France and accepted the appointment for the following year.

For several months, Bobby was traveling around the country, visiting churches to seek support for our mission. I remained in Shreveport, preparing for our trip and dealing with dad.

He felt lost during this time, and I realized how dependant he had been on my mother. She had been ill for so long, weak and fragile for so many years, and yet she was his rock.

But once my decision was made, I was at peace. That's not to say I wasn't concerned for my father, but I knew my Heavenly Father would find a way to look after him while I was away.

Dad would often stop by our house and beg me not to leave. It was strange to see my father in such a state for the first time. He was a big man, always sure-footed and strong, a hunter and fisherman who had always taken care of my mother and his family. And here he was, really struggling with the thought of being on his own.

My brothers would be there for him, of course, but in the months when I had been taking care of mother I saw how he needed a woman in his life.

One day he was particularly insistent and cried when he asked me not to go, and once again could not be persuaded by my assurances that God would look after him. I was a little exasperated, and finally I said, "You'll meet someone."

As soon as the words came out of my mouth I knew it was true. I was suddenly as sure as I'd ever been about anything that this was the way the Lord would look after my father. I knew the Lord would provide him with a companion.

"Who?" he demanded.

I think the very idea both shocked and intrigued him. I'm not sure the thought had crossed his mind before that moment that he might one day remarry.

"Whatever happened to Lois McQuillen?" I asked.

Lois was the mother of one of my high school friends, and her name just popped into my head. I had not thought of her in quite some time, and had no idea where she was.

About a week went by, and I hadn't heard a word from my father since that conversation. Suddenly he called out of the blue to ask if I'd come over at five o'clock. I said I would, and he hung up. It was a little unusual, as he had gotten into the habit of just dropping by, but I thought maybe it had begun to sink in that I was leaving and he was trying to get used to the idea of separation.

When I arrived, my brothers were there, and I immediately assumed we would all go out for supper, but they both had funny little smiles on their faces. Before I could quiz them about what was going on, my father asked to speak with me privately. Puzzled, I followed him into the den, where he told me that he had a date that night with Lois McQuillen, and he wanted my blessing!

Now I understood why my brothers were smiling. Daddy had called all three of his children over about fifteen minutes apart so he could speak with each of us individually to break the news of his outing.

After he strutted out the door, looking quite dapper in his brand-new suit, there was a brief moment of stunned silence before we all burst into hearty laughter. I don't think any of us expected that!

Of course we were all terribly pleased, because he looked as happy as he'd been in quite some time. We had all seen how devastated he was after the death of my mother, and it was a joy to see him with a spring in his step again. Even so, none of us suspected his life would change so quickly, and in such a dramatic fashion.

Dad and Lois were married in April, two months before I left for France, and he was so head-over-heels in love I'm not even sure he was aware I'd gone until he received my first letter from overseas. Needless to say, this was quite a change from him begging me not to go, and Bobby and I were quite amused by it all.

Of course I'm exaggerating just a little at Dad's reaction when we left, but not by much. He was just so completely taken with his new bride that not much else got his attention. It was really very sweet to see him and Lois so much in love and acting like newlyweds, which of course they were.

The point is that he was doing well, and in the care of the Lord (and Lois!).

Bobby and I were so grateful to God for putting the two of them together at the perfect time in their lives, and ours.

So, it had been quite a year, filled with both hope and sorrow.

I felt the Lord's call to serve overseas in October.

In December, my mother passed.

In April, Dad remarried.

Bobby and I moved to France in June.

It was another reminder the Lord has His hand on us in all things.

He is with us in sadness; He is with us in joy.

We need only accept His will for our lives.

30
ATTACKED, BUT NOT DESTROYED

Sacrifice

"Be strong and courageous. Do not be afraid or terrified because of them, for the LORD your God goes with you; he will never leave you nor forsake you."
Deuteronomy 31:6

Just before 11:00 P.M. on the evening of October 10, 2006, I was awakened by what was probably the loudest explosion I'd ever heard. It was so loud, as a matter of fact, that I assumed at first a rocket had landed right next to my trailer. The entire modular building shook with the force of the blast.

It was confusing at first, because although it seemed like it exploded right next door, there was no flash of light through the windows, as was the case whenever incoming or outgoing fire was nearby.

For an instant I was petrified, but it quickly passed and I rolled out of bed, saying a silent prayer practically before I hit the floor. I am always amazed by how the Lord strengthens us to endure and adapt in trying times.

No matter how bad things get, no matter how fearful we become, the Lord will always be there to help us through it.

> "Be strong and of a good courage, fear not, nor be afraid of them: for the Lord your God, He it is that does go with you; He will not fail you, nor forsake you."

Deuteronomy 31:6

He will not fail you, nor forsake you.

What a powerful feeling, to know deep down that there is a wonderful, loving God who is always there for you. Many times we will find ourselves in circumstances where His presence is not readily apparent, except through faith. But our faith will always see us through. And that faith comes from God.

"We live by faith, not by sight." - 2 Corinthians 5:7.

So after that huge explosion, when I had no idea what had happened, when there was nothing to show me what might happen next, when I rolled out of bed and hugged the floor, I did the only thing I could. The only thing I needed to do. I spoke to the Lord.

Prayer has long been second nature to me, but that instinct was, of course, intensified during my time in Iraq.

I lay there in complete silence for several moments before I heard the buzz of new activity outside. As I've mentioned, there was always noise, mostly the steady rumble of trucks passing on roads nearby as soldiers came and went, but now I heard the voices of others who were also awakened by the enormous blast.

What no one knew for certain until the next day was that Camp Falcon, a large ammunition storage dump just south of Baghdad, had taken a direct hit of mortar fire, which ignited a large supply of tank, artillery, and small arms ordnance.

With all the 'burn off' of the ammunition, things were quite chaotic, as you would imagine.

Smaller explosions continued for the next several hours, and the fire was still burning the next morning. It was felt all over Baghdad, and the experience was likely similar to the initial bombing at the start of the war in 2003. Some initially thought it might have even been a tactical nuclear device which had exploded, but of course that was not the case. It does, however, give you an idea of the magnitude of the blast.

Many buildings in the area were completely destroyed and Camp Falcon was in shambles, but there were no casualties save for a few minor injuries! I praised the Lord for the miracle of His protection in the midst of such destruction.

An MWR supervisor there, Jozette Jenkins, had spoken with me only a week prior, expressing serious concerns about returning to Camp Falcon after an R and R, during which her daughter had a disturbing dream about her mother's safety. I can only imagine what must have been going through her mind to be right in the middle of all that during the night. The workers there spent the rest of that night sleeping on the ground (if they slept at all) because their trailers had all been destroyed.

There were many others with whom I worked who sacrificed even more.

Just a few days prior to the large attack on Camp Falcon, one of the MWR technicians there, a wonderful young man named Randy McBroom with whom I communicated daily, was injured terribly by a mortar attack just outside the fitness center. All of the camps were attacked on a daily basis, with mortars and rockets aimed over the walls from the surrounding areas.

Randy had just stepped outside after carrying supplies into the center when a rocket hit the facility.

Fortunately he wasn't killed, but he spent many months in hospitals recovering from his injuries, enduring painful physical therapy before he could walk again.

Thankfully, he remembered nothing at all about the attack, and to this day retains his sunny disposition in spite of all the difficulties he went through. I am in awe of his sacrifice.

Three days later, the entire camp where he worked was destroyed.

The military ascertained the mortar which set off the Camp Falcon munitions had been fired from Abu Dsheer, a mostly Shiite area in the Sunni district of Dora, which was a notably troubled area.

It had the distinction of being the site of the very first bombing engagement, just prior to the start of the war. It was the area where Saddam Hussein was believed to be visiting at the time with his sons, Uday and Qusay.

Dora had a population of several hundred thousand people, many of whom were Christian. As a matter of fact, it was home to one of the largest Christian communities in Iraq. Many Americans are surprised by this, but yes, there are many Christians in Iraq.

After the death and resurrection of Jesus, the apostle Thomas traveled east to spread the gospel, throughout Mesopotamia and all the way to India.

Christians have lived in Iraq ever since. But the last several years have seen much persecution by Al Qaeda and Shiite militias, and the Christian population has suffered greatly. As I write this in the fall of 2008, there have been reports of Christians being persecuted by Sunnis in the northern section of Iraq near Mosul.

Even so, there are still Christians throughout the region who risk their lives to worship, and they need and deserve our support.

We in the United States sometimes forget how easy it is to practice our faith. Most of us probably live within a few miles of a church (if that), and yet how often do we sleep in on Sunday morning or sit on the couch on Wednesday evening watching television, when so many others must actually put their lives on the line to enter the house of the Lord?

What a privilege it is to openly worship God!

If the story of my experiences in Iraq reminds even a single person to thank the Lord for this, the first of His many blessings, I will be forever grateful. And those Christians in Iraq remind us all of the glory of His message. I am privileged, also, to write of them now.

So even in Dora, where mortars are fired in an attempt to kill our soldiers, where Christians are persecuted and killed for worshipping Christ, in the center of the Islamic world, where Saddam Hussein once ruled in tyranny, the Word of God is still heard.

For those who question our mission in Iraq, I wish they could see what I've seen, and witness the sacrifices of so many in the service of the freedom we hold so dear.

Sacrifice comes in many forms. From a mother calming the concerns of her worried child, to a young man learning how to walk again, to the Christians who risk their life to worship, to the brave soldiers who protect them all, each one is blessed in the eyes of the Lord, who understands what sacrifice means.

> "For God so loved the world that He gave his only begotten Son, that whosoever believeth in Him should not perish, but have everlasting life."

> – John 3:16

31
GOD IS IN CONTROL

Peace

"Be still, and know that I am God; I will be exalted among the nations, I will be exalted in the earth."
Psalm 46:10

We arrived in France in the summer of 1973, and settled just outside Versailles. As the first missionaries ever sent to France by the United Pentecostal Church, Bobby and I both felt a real seriousness of purpose which this endeavor required. At the same time, we were almost giddy with excitement. We felt like our entire lives had prepared us for this moment, and looked forward eagerly to the challenges ahead.

Even after the whirlwind of the past several years, it felt peaceful to pack up our two children and travel halfway across the globe to spread the word of God as missionaries for the UPC.

That peace came from the certainty that once more, we were right where the Lord wanted us to be. Bobby had wanted to return to France practically from the day we left, but I had resisted. However, when I felt the tug of the Holy Spirit months before, everything fell into place and we both knew the time was right.

Our son Byron started school there at the age of two, which was a great age to learn a new language. He was practically bi-lingual from the time he started talking, and eventually sounded just like a native. Bren was nine and had, of course, been in school in the States, but he also adapted very well.

Back in those days communication with our families was relatively rare. We were not making much money, so a brief telephone call to the U.S. a couple of times a month was all we could afford. But we wrote often and loved receiving cards and letters in return.

It's amazing now to think of computers and cell phones and text messages that exist today and which make staying in touch so much easier.

Bobby quickly developed a teaching program with twenty-one 'preaching points, and began traveling throughout France, teaching many fine young men to become ministers.

Sometimes he would hold meetings in churches, sometimes in private homes. Wherever there was a need and a willing body, Bobby would go there and minister.

And he truly loved the work. Bobby had a real affinity for young people, and had excelled back in Shreveport as a youth minister. He had such a vibrant personality that really appealed to them, and they related to his wisdom and experience in a way that made him a worthy role model. I watched him grow as a teacher almost daily.

I watched when he held Bible study for the other soldiers, some no older than himself and some much older, during our first stay in France. I watched him preach to crowds large and small. Yet I was continually impressed as he matured more and more into the fine preacher he became.

He had such curiosity and a real hunger for knowledge that others found infectious, and as I watched him grow in his faith I was immeasurably proud.

I, too, was growing, both spiritually and emotionally. I began to truly understand what my mother had accomplished in raising me and my brothers, as well as being a good wife to my father, and I rededicated myself to following in her footsteps as both Bobby and I continued to dedicate our lives to the Lord.

My boys were a treasure. I went to school to learn French, and their immersion into the language and culture made me work even harder to catch up. They were both developing their own unique personalities, and it was a joy to watch them become friends as well as brothers, in spite of their age difference.

I remembered how Bren had asked to 'give his brother back' a few days after Byron was born, and I can't tell you how happy I was that now, such a thought was the furthest thing from his mind. Never overestimate the blessing of children who actually enjoy each other's company.

The Alpha Training Course adopted by the UPC was a three year program designed to train the next generation of preachers to serve all over France. I was put to work typing up the course materials, which would then be sent to the United States for printing.

Once a year, Bobby would hold a conference for young people all over Europe, which lasted two weeks and was as spiritually uplifting for us as it was the participants.

To see so many young people eager to learn about Christ and anxious to spread the Gospel was awesome and inspiring. We looked forward to that time each year, and prepared for months, in addition to our other work.

We always had so much to do, so many things to accomplish, and yet we never felt too rushed, or pressed for time. It was exhausting, but with our labors came a great peace of knowing that we were doing exactly what the Lord wanted us to do.

I cooked all the time, often preparing meals for twenty people or more. Bobby loved to entertain, and often the conversations lasted long after I put the boys in bed for the night.

We had so many wonderful friends, people who loved the Lord and shared our passion for service. Our days were filled with hard work, love, and laughter, and our time there was extraordinarily fulfilling.

One day a week we reserved for family time, and would take the boys to explore a particular area or visit a new museum, or go for a picnic in the park.

Bobby would always have wonderful stories and information for the boys about what we saw, and I could see him infusing his sons with curiosity and a love for knowledge. At times it reminded me of our trip to the Holy Land, when Bobby would lead us on tours of the area, having prepared meticulously for each day's adventures.

Every now and then I got the giggles thinking back to our long trip in the Bug as I watched him with the boys, and he would wink and call me 'Baby-doll,' which always made me blush.

For the first two years of our marriage, Bobby called me 'kid.' I didn't know why. There's something about men and nicknames.

I actually never much cared for 'kid,' but he said it with such affection I never corrected him.

Once when my guard was down, I admitted to him my feeling for that particular term of endearment. Rather than be hurt, or ask me why I'd never told him, Bobby just smiled and said, "Okay, baby-doll."

We just looked at each other and burst into giggles, and that was what he called me for the next nineteen years. Sometimes he shortened it to 'doll,' but the way he said it always made me smile.

Even today, whenever I hear someone say 'doll,' it fills my heart with happy memories.

Bobby was a wonderful husband and father, and we were doing the work of the Lord. Our time in France as missionaries, were truly the happiest years of my life.

The term of service was for four years, but three months before we were scheduled to return, we got word that Bobby's mother was dying of cancer.

I flew back to the States immediately with Byron, and Bobby quickly finished all our business there and followed soon after with Bren.

Doris Dykes, unlike my own mother, had always been very healthy, and it was a shock to everyone when the doctor told us how little time she had left.

She and I had always enjoyed a very close relationship. She had been with Bobby that day in the market in Mexico when he first realized he was in love with me, and she had endured the non-stop drive to Louisiana as her love-sick son rushed back to tell me.

She had always known Bobby and I were meant for each other, and I loved her for that.

Doris was a wonderful Christian, patient and kind, and always knew just the right thing to say. If for any reason I was unable to speak with my own mother, I knew Doris would be right there if I needed to talk.

I considered her a real friend, and we got along wonderfully. There was never any of the stereotypical mother-in-law tension between us. Just as my own mother doted on Bobby, Doris treated me as if I were her own daughter. There was a real comfortableness between us. Bobby and I were lucky to have such wise and understanding in-laws. Doris was a model for how I later dealt with my own sons' wives.

During her last few weeks, it was a difficult time, but we were so very grateful for those last days with her. When she passed away, she was at peace with the Lord and surrounded by those who loved her.

During the time when we first heard of Doris' illness and left France to be with her, I noticed my hands would shake dramatically whenever I tried to write. I could barely even sign my name, and Bobby would have to help me even signing a check.

After a few months, this strange manifestation disappeared, but would return occasionally during particularly stressful periods of my life. I was a little embarrassed by this, and shared it only with my immediate family, who would come to my aid for thank you notes and the like.

There are so many things in life we don't understand, but I am comforted to know that God is in control of it all.

Bobby and I spent that summer traveling the country, visiting churches and speaking of our experiences as missionaries. We both loved to share and enjoyed meeting new people. Bobby especially enjoyed talking to the crowds. That man was born to preach. There was no doubt about it.

During this time, we talked about whether to apply for another four year assignment. Bobby was considering applying to France, but the UPC had another posting in mind. Bobby had done such a good job there that the UPC had more applicants than they could send to France.

They wanted to send us to the Ivory Coast, Madagascar or Haiti; other French speaking countries where UPC missionaries were needed, but the First Pentecostal Church of Slidell, Louisiana contacted Bobby about taking the pastorate there.

We prayed about it, and decided to stay in the United States and accept the job.

The church had a new and vibrant congregation and Bobby felt they were ready to grow, so it was an exciting prospect for both of us.

Both of us were happy to settle down once again and start the next chapter of our lives in service of the Lord.

We moved to Slidell in August of 1977, and the church was everything we expected. The congregation was welcoming and enthusiastic, and we thought it was a place we could stay for a long time.

As we moved in, we talked and talked. Bobby really was my best friend. We discussed the church, and the schools, the neighborhood, and the future. We felt centered and secure. Everything seemed right. As happy as we had been in France, we were looking forward to many more years of the same.

Once more, our future seemed to be laid out before us, as clean and smooth as a ribbon on glass. We didn't know where He would lead us, but we were confident in our journey.

We thought we might be comfortable there in Slidell for many years, or we could be ready at a moment's notice if the Lord called us to another church. Many pastors stay in the same church home their entire career, while others continually accept new challenges, new churches, new congregations.

The important thing was we were ready.

The last several years were like a baptism by fire for us, and after all we'd been through, all the places we'd been, we really believed we were ready for whatever the Lord had in store.

But as I've said before, we never know what the Lord has in store for us.

The Slidell First United Pentecostal Church would be Bobby's last pastorate.

In just three years, the Lord would take him home.

Never again would I see his smile, hear his voice, or feel the warm touch of his embrace. But I knew Bobby was in a better place, with his Lord and Savior, Jesus Christ.

"Precious in the sight of the Lord is the death of his saints."

- Psalms 116:15.

We can never know what's around the next corner. We can never assume even one more day with those we love.

But we can take comfort in knowing that God is in control of it all.

32

THE LIGHT WITHIN BAGHDAD

Fellowship

As iron sharpens iron,
so one man sharpens another
Proverbs 27:17

Routine can be very comforting. No matter where we are, or what we're doing, the familiarity of even the simplest of tasks reminds us who we are and where we come from. It keeps us grounded, even in the midst of turmoil and strife. In good times and bad, we eat, we sleep, and we do all the little things on a daily basis which form the routine of our lives.

Routine also serves to remind us of our common humanity. All of the things we share as human beings and all our commonalities contribute to who we are. In spite of all our misunderstandings, we are not so different in the eyes of the Lord. Each person on earth is a singular child of God, created in His image, and as such we are all blessed creatures.

As children, we all start with the same trusting nature, eager to learn, and love, and with the capacity to accept all the good things God wants for us. All He asks is that we come to Him.

"Red and yellow, black and white, they are precious in his sight, Jesus loves the little children of the world." These lyrics, of course, are from the simple yet beautiful hymn by C. Herbert Woolsten and George F. Root, based on the words of Jesus in Matthew 19:14: "Let the little children come to me, and do not hinder them, for the kingdom of heaven belongs to such as these."

All of us are His children, and we all must come to Him as a child, with simple trust and faith. Once we accept Jesus as our Lord and Savior, and are born again, we then begin to build a personal relationship, establishing a life in service of His name.

As a Christian, part of my daily routine must always be the simple act of prayer, which not only keeps me in touch with God and provides spiritual comfort, but helps remind me that, no matter what, He is always there for me, just as He is for anyone who calls His name.

It is amazing to me how anyone can go through a single day without once communicating with the Lord. Prayer has provided succor and solace throughout my life, and that was especially true during my time in Iraq.

And just as we need to pray, I believe also that God needs to hear our voice.

Imagine how a parent feels after a long day without once hearing the sound of their child's voice. As a mother I know how wonderful it is to hear my children call my name. I can't imagine life without the memory of their sweet voices, and how they've changed over the years as they've grown into adults.

But no matter how old they get, they are always and forever my children. It never ends. And as their mother I will always desire to hear them call my name. Just as I comforted them from the time they were babies, so now do their voices comfort me.

And so, too, does the Lord desire to hear our voice. We are always and forever His children, and He wants to hear from us. Not just when times are bad, but every day.

It's easy to call on God when we need something, or are frightened, or threatened. But we must also share with Him our joys. He will be there, of course, in times of need, but what parent doesn't rejoice to hear of their children's happiness, too? What parent doesn't want to hear of their child's joy as well?

That's why we must share it all with Him. The good and the bad; when we're happy, when we're sad. Our burdens will be lighter and our joys will be higher. And we share through our prayer.

Our voices, as His children, bring comfort and joy to our Lord and Savior.

Think about that for a moment. There is actually something we can do on a daily basis that brings real joy to our Heavenly Father. What an awesome idea!

This is why I simply love to pray. I love to speak to my Lord, and it brings me such joy to know that He not only hears me, but enjoys our time together just as much as I do. That is a wonderful feeling, to know that such a simple part of my daily routine can accomplish so much. Each day in Baghdad when I awoke and said my morning prayers, it made the coming day's tasks seem much less daunting.

There's really no such thing as a 'typical' day in Iraq, but there is, underneath everything else, a routine to follow. It was often interrupted, but it was there as the foundation of my workday, and it kept me focused on my duties just as prayer keeps me focused spiritually.

Typically, I would rise at 5:30 A.M. Breakfast was available at the DFAC, but over time I began to keep breakfast foods in my room so I could eat there before heading out to the office.

When you work fifteen hours a day, every quiet moment is precious, and I enjoyed the peaceful 'alone time' before I started my day.

The office was just a three minute walk, and I would usually arrive at 7:00 A.M. Most of the other staff would take that time to have breakfast at the DFAC or go the cleaners (dust, dust, dust), so I would use the time to speak with the regional director prior to the daily 8:00 A.M. staff meeting, during which our itinerary and schedule for the day would be determined.

By 9:00 A.M., the reports from other sites and facilities would flood in. Usually my assistant would compile roughly twenty-two reports from the facilities into one report for me to look over, which I would then verify for the director of services.

The monthly calendar of events and services would also be compiled and sent to the military for verification.

During all this, the phone would constantly ring with personnel issues or facility problems which needed attention. Budgets were prepared, equipment was discussed and ordered, either locally or internationally, and then that request was forwarded to others for approval.

There was a constant inflow of new hires needing time and attention, as well as repair technicians and other staff whose comings and goings had to be coordinated in terms of transportation.

And, of course, all of this could be interrupted by incoming or outgoing fire, or both. You never knew when there would be an explosion of some kind.

Just a typical busy day at a medium to large-sized corporation in the middle of a war zone!

My routine in Iraq was a comfort to me. While it could vary or be interrupted or even scrapped altogether, depending on the circumstances, it was the foundation upon which I based my work.

It was familiar and solid, and I depended on that routine to do my job.

My routine, and the routines of thousands of others like me, combined to contribute to the entire effort in Iraq. Each of us was an essential part of the whole, and important in our own small way.

As Christians, we are also part of a great effort. An effort to spread the Word of God. Our relationship with Jesus is our foundation, and our routine is daily prayer. Just imagine the joy God receives from millions of believers all over the world, raising their voices in unison to their Heavenly Father.

Just as in Baghdad, our lives are often interrupted by unforeseen circumstances. But we can take comfort in our routine of daily communication with God. No matter where we are, or what we're doing, we can always stop and speak directly to our Lord.

Just tell Him what you're feeling, and He will always listen.

On a daily basis in Iraq, I asked the Lord to allow others to see God through me and my actions. I prayed constantly to be filled with the Holy Spirit, and asked that God allow others to benefit from that blessing as well.

It wasn't for my own aggrandizement, but because my relationship with the Lord was so wonderful I simply had to share it as much as I possibly could.

It's as if you were told the most wonderful story you'd ever heard, and couldn't wait to share it with everyone you met.

I prayed daily for the Light of Jesus to shine through me. I believe God's presence can provide peace and comfort even in the midst of war, and I wanted to be a vessel for Christ's goodness.

One day when I was shopping in a crowded PX, not really noticing any of my fellow patrons, just focused on the particular item I was looking for, I was approached by a man I did not know.

"Praise the Lord, I have finally found you!" he exclaimed.

I was surprised, but I responded, "Praise the Lord."

"When I opened the door to the PX, I sensed the presence of the Lord, and I've been searching the aisles to find you."

We shared for a bit before going our separate ways. It was a moving experience and validation that God's Spirit is a very real presence in our lives. I was deeply humbled by this incident, and had similar experiences during my time in Iraq when strangers sought me out to share their faith.

I am grateful to God for allowing His light to shine through me, and give all glory to His name.

Of all my life lessons, this is the one to which I must continually return, and perhaps the most enduring:

No matter where we are or what's happening in our lives, God's light will shine through, providing peace and the comfort that all is well, because He is always in control.

33

TAPESTRY OF LIFE

Grief

Brothers, we do not want you to be ignorant about those who fall asleep, or to grieve like the rest of men, who have no hope. We believe that Jesus died and rose again and so we believe that God will bring with Jesus those who have fallen asleep in him.
1 Thessalonians 4:13-14

I rolled over in bed and draped my arm across Bobby, snuggling closer. For some reason I felt cold, though it was near the end of a typically hot Louisiana summer. I felt no warmth as I usually did whenever I ventured onto my husband's side of the bed in the night, and opened my eyes.

But Bobby wasn't there.

My beloved husband had died in a tragic accident, a victim, so said the official report, of a shaft collapse at the bottom of a gold mine.

I cried until the sun came up. It would be months before I was able to sleep more than a couple of hours at a time. Before I could bring myself to sleep on his side of the bed to avoid waking in the middle of the night reaching for him. Before every waking moment wasn't filled with my restless inner voice screaming, "He's gone!"

Eventually I came to understand the Lord had been preparing me for Bobby's death for some time.

Five months before the accident, I dreamt three nights in a row that Mom Dykes, Bobby's wonderful mother whom we lost three years prior, was calling for her son.

Three months before he died, Bobby encouraged me to take up my music again, going so far as to rent a saxophone for me to practice with. He knew how much I loved music, but our lives had been so busy these last years it was easy to let such things fall by the wayside. Perhaps Bobby blamed himself for the lapse, and I can't help but think if he sensed his life was going to take a different path somehow, he would have wanted to provide every possible avenue for my happiness before he left.

The events during the week leading up to his death also later confirmed my understanding the Lord was preparing me for his loss.

On the Sunday morning before his death, Bobby wept as he asked for the congregation's prayers for the protective hand of the Lord, and the presence of the Holy Spirit was deeply felt. It was a different type of sermon from how Bobby normally preached, and I remember the strong feelings from the members.

The evening service that night was quite joyful, and Bobby baptized four believers in Jesus' name. The portents of the morning seemed far away that night.

The next day, Bobby and I had a particularly emotional talk. There were many reminiscences and closely held feelings not often scrutinized. Our lives to that point had been full, enough for several lifetimes and there were things Bobby seemed especially eager to share.

As we prayed together, Bobby asked the Lord to protect me in his absence. The next day, he left for Idaho. As I stood watching until his plane was out of sight, I couldn't help feeling a sense of desperation, as if I would never see him again.

A week later, Bobby was dead.

On Thursday of that week, I had lunch with a friend, and we spoke of our husbands. I commented my hope to never lose Bobby, because I would not only be losing my best friend and partner, but also my pastor.

As the wife of a preacher, my place in the church was defined by my husband. I knew I would lose not only my soul-mate, but also my church home.

It was a strange conversation, and I wasn't exactly sure where my words were coming from. In spite of all my feelings and intuition, it was almost as if my mind could not conceive what my heart was telling me. Perhaps the Lord was protecting me, gently preparing me for the coming days.

I anxiously awaited Bobby's prearranged phone call on Friday evening, and we spoke for over an hour. I related a conversation I'd had the previous day with a member of our church, who had a vision of Bobby surrounded by gold. Bobby interpreted this as the 'streets of gold' to be found in Heaven, but seemed unconcerned about the possible implication of that explanation.

Was this a premonition of his ascent into glory? Or did the vision symbolize Bobby's death in a mine of gold? Regardless, I was feeling increasingly uneasy.

He told me he was going to stay for a few more days, and a substitute pastor would be arriving for the coming weekend's services.

Bobby and I had purchased the claim on an old mine in Idaho from a tenant in our rental house named Gary Robins. We placed a trailer on the property in which he could stay while performing various tasks, such as taking samples and delivering them to the local assayer's office.

But Gary had not been doing the work, so Bobby needed to stay and finish the job before returning. He sounded put out, so I tried to sound supportive in spite of my worry.

The following Sunday afternoon, I suddenly had a terrible feeling. I needed to speak to Bobby. I called his motel, but he was not in his room. Unknown to me at the time, I had called at the very hour of his death.

At the evening service, as the visiting minister called the saints of the church to prayer for their pastor, I was unmoved, believing there was no longer a need for such a prayer. It was a very strange feeling, one which I couldn't explain, as I did not yet know Bobby was dead.

After the service, my sons and I met the visiting minister and his wife at a local restaurant for a meal. We arrived late, and they finished their meal before us. They offered to stay until we were also finished, but I told them it wasn't necessary. Unspoken in my mind was the fact I would have to get used to being alone with my boys.

As I walked to the car with my arms around my sons Bren, 16, and Byron, 9, I could hardly believe what I was thinking. It was almost as if I did know, and the Lord had me on automatic pilot to enable me to get through the next hours.

After a fitful night, the doorbell rang at 6:45 A.M. and I knew.

My mind caught up with my heart, and I opened the door to two policemen, who informed me Bobby was dead.

Even though I was grateful for the Lord's preparation to that point, every fiber of my being cried out in agony for my loss.

The next days were miserable. I broke the news to my sons, who were devastated, of course. It was a shock to us all, and we were in a state of disbelief. It was three days before Bobby's body was returned to me.

But the Lord was with me constantly, providing many comforts. On Tuesday evening a group of ministers and friends knelt around my bed and prayed to the Lord for my rest and reassurance. As I lay there trying to sleep, I saw my mother, long passed, looking as beautiful and radiant as I'd ever seen her in life. She extended her arms and smiled, saying to someone unseen, "So good to see you!"

At that moment, I knew without a doubt that my mother had just welcomed Bobby into Heaven, and everything would be all right.

That memory has always been a source of strength and inspiration for me. From that moment on I have felt real peace within, which has lasted my entire life.

With blessed assurance I know one day I will greet them both the same way.

Still, it was extremely difficult. Losing a spouse is never easy. As hard as you think it will be, you can only pray it's that easy. Like so many trials in life, you must give it up to God and allow Him to show you the way.

I sought comfort in the Bible, and found this passage to be especially enlightening:

"Although the fig tree shall not blossom, neither shall fruit be in the vines; the labor of the olive shall fail, and the fields shall yield no meat; the flock shall be cut off from the fold, and there shall be no herd in the stalls: Yet I will rejoice in the Lord, I will joy in the God of my salvation. The Lord God is my strength, and He will make my feet like hinds' feet, and He will make to walk upon mine high places." – Habakkuk 3:17-19.

Few days have passed since that difficult time that I have not derived strength and courage from those verses.

Just as my conversation over lunch on the Thursday before his death foretold, my life was to drastically change without Bobby.

As the wife of a minister, I no longer had a church in which to pour my energies. Obviously a new pastor would be needed, and my continued presence would only serve as a reminder of where the church had been, instead of where it needed to go.

Of course, no one would have ever asked me to leave, but I knew it would be better for the next pastor, so I made plans to find another church home. I also thought the boys would benefit from our return to Shreveport, where my family lived.

We had a new house, a new church, a new environment, old friendships renewed. It was like a whole new world. It felt like the right thing to do.

But I was as scared as I'd ever been.

Since I was a teenager, I had been with Bobby. And here I was, a widow at forty, missing my best friend for the first time in a lifetime. I felt deformed; part of me was gone.

I had given myself totally to Bobby, emotionally and physically. Could I make it on my own? Could I raise my boys without their father? So many questions, so many changes. What was I to do?

I felt isolated and helpless. These feelings are not easily overcome, but I prayed for guidance and tried to be patient with myself. I knew the healing process would be long and difficult.

The boys and I had our ups and downs. There were good days and bad. But I felt the presence of the Lord, and knew His protection would endure.

Church was actually the most difficult for me. It was some time before I could get through a service without expecting to see Bobby up there preaching. Holidays and anniversaries were also hard, but often the grief would hit when I least expected it.

It might be a song on the radio, or a picture in a magazine. Almost anything could trigger a memory of a long forgotten moment we shared, and the grief was overwhelming.

I read the Bible constantly, and scoured book stores for anything which might help. Being a widow at forty didn't seem right. It was a label more appropriate for those much older than me.

Years later in Iraq, I felt deeply for those left behind when a soldier died, knowing the pain and grief to be felt by so many women even younger than I was back then.

I desperately wanted someone to talk to, someone my own age who had gone through the same thing. This also helped me when I dealt with the soldiers in Iraq. It's amazing how our life's journey is preparation for all that comes after.

My own experiences with the death of my mother and mother-in-law were helpful in many ways for dealing with Bobby's loss, especially during that first year.

I had a very difficult time after my mother's death. Bobby was on deputation, and so I relied on a good friend who listened and cried with me. When I was reunited with Bobby in France, he held me every night for months as I cried myself to sleep.

But he was patient and kind, and I often remembered his words during the time after his death. Bobby was a strong person, and he believed grief was often feeling sorry for oneself. As believers, we understand death is not the end, but a continuation of our earthly journey. I knew my husband was in a better place.

Bobby helped me understand my feelings were perfectly normal after my mother's death, and his wisdom helped me after his own passing.

But I never would have made it through that first year without my faith. God was with me every step of the way, His presence a constant reminder that I would make it through to the other side of my pain and grief.

I also depended on my family and many dear friends around the world.

I began to keep notebooks of my thoughts. I wrote down a goal for each day, as well as long term goals, with a devotional section in which I recorded parts of Bobby's last sermons. These things warmed my heart and inspired my soul.

Gradually, I began to understand I could not simply shut myself away, so I joined a group of Christian women for regular health club visits. This provided both fellowship and fitness, easing my tension and allowing me to take my mind off things for a time.

I forced myself to go to meetings and conferences which I had previously attended with Bobby. It was difficult, and I often felt awkward, both for myself and for those with whom I came in contact.

I didn't want to face these people who only knew me as Bobby's wife, but I soldiered on. I know it was difficult for them, too.

It's hard to be around pain, suffering, and grief. Wanting to help but not knowing what to say or do. This also prepared for what I later experienced in Iraq.

When I lost Bobby, I wanted to be acknowledged. I didn't want anyone to turn away. I needed to talk. There was so much inside that needed to come out.

I wanted to talk about the times we shared, the experiences we had together. Bobby was a huge part of my life, and it hurt when that part of me was ignored.

The happiest times of my life were the years we spent as missionaries in France. I remember standing with him one day in a beautiful chateau, admiring an exquisite tapestry. But as we approached, it was clear the tapestry was just a collection of knots and threads.

My life felt like that tapestry. I had so many beautiful experiences with Bobby, but in my grief I was looking at things differently, feeling sorry for myself and forgetting the beauty.

I needed to get to the point once more where I could step back and see the tapestry as I once beheld it. I needed to get past my grief and appreciate my life with Bobby once again for what it was, the most beautiful time in my life.

All of us experience loss, and we will each handle grief in different ways. But through the grace of God we can find our way through.

It may seem insurmountable, but the Lord will provide the strength we need at the right time. As long as we put our trust in the Him, He'll show us the way. And we'll come out on the other side as a beautiful tapestry in spite of the knots and threads along the way.

In the words of David, "Thou hast turned for me my mourning into dancing: thou hast put off my sackcloth, and girded me with gladness." – Psalms 30:11

I am forever grateful to God for the tapestry which was my life with Bobby.

34
OPERATION IRAQI SALVATION

Freedom

[31] To the Jews who had believed him, Jesus said, "If you hold to my teaching, you are really my disciples. [32] Then you will know the truth, and the truth will set you free."
John 8:31-32

Just as the Lord gives us strength as individuals to overcome trying times and come through on the other side as stronger persons, so do I believe the Lord will strengthen the United States after our difficult times in Iraq.

I am extremely proud to have done my small part to support our troops there. In spite of the criticisms after the initial invasion, I fervently believe our efforts will have many long-lasting and positive effects on the region, and consequently, the world.

I believe God has His hand on us as a nation, and though the obstacles in this particular endeavor have seemed almost insurmountable at times, there is nothing we cannot do as a people as long as we put our faith in Him.

I am proud to say that the level of violence in Iraq since I was there is way down, and security is improving with each passing day.

As someone who was there in the beginning, when I hear of the improvements being made, I am filled with pride for our brave soldiers and the commanders who watch over them. I only wish more Americans heard of the progress, also.

There have been many dark times, but we must remain steadfast when our work is worthwhile, and who can argue that bringing democracy to Iraq and freeing the people from the dictator Saddam Hussein wasn't a worthwhile pursuit?

As Americans we have gotten used to instant gratification; every conceivable need can be quickly met. We consume fast food, we have our oil changed in thirty minutes, and we race through the checkout line at the supermarket with fifteen items or less in time to arrive home for our favorite television show, which is also available on the internet if we decide the scheduled time is inconvenient to our busy lives.

There are video games, i-pods, and cell phones that do everything but answer themselves. We enjoy instant communications with friends around the globe, and the technological advances come so fast of late that it's difficult for all but the very young to keep up.

With such realities in our society, it's no wonder many Americans have become impatient during this war.

But it's important to understand not just how large a task we have undertaken, but also how much we have already accomplished toward meeting the goal of a free and stable Iraq.

The war is a microcosm of the larger fight against Islamic terrorism, and every battle on every street directly affects our security as a nation, as well as that of our allies and the entire free world. Our task is as basic as protecting the right of all people to live and speak and worship freely, and what is more essential than that?

For those who want to leave before our mission is accomplished, I would say this: We simply cannot walk away from the front lines of such an important job when nothing less than the security of the free world is at stake.

And we have accomplished much, in spite of the resistance in much of the mainstream media to inform the American people of such progress.

It is particularly grieving to see our accomplishments go unreported when so many have sacrificed so much to realize those accomplishments, as well as protecting the right of the press to report on them.

Thousands of schools have been renovated, and hundreds more are being built. There are now dozens of universities and other institutes of higher learning open and operating in Iraq, including medical research facilities, and females are now allowed to attend, which was not always true.

Over four million Iraqi children were enrolled in primary school by 2006, and Iraqi students are now studying in the U.S. on Fulbright scholarships.

96% of Iraqi children under five have received polio vaccinations, a statistic we take for granted but something which, if ignored, could decimate a society in the event of an outbreak.

Iraq now has an operational navy and air force, and tens of thousands of police officers have been equipped and trained for domestic service to their countrymen, with several police academies turning out more every day. How many of us would want to live in a place where we couldn't count on police protection when we needed it?

So many things are taken for granted in western countries which are just now being realized in Iraq due to the hard work of the U.S. and its allies.

Railway stations, hospitals, utility and water facilities have all been built, and more are under construction with each passing day.

There are at least seventy-five radio stations and a dozen television stations, as well as nearly two hundred newspapers.

Everything that makes a nation a nation is being created in Iraq by coalition forces, all while fighting a war!

Almost fifty countries have re-established embassies in Iraq, with more to come, and al-Qaeda in Iraq is on the run.

General David Petraeus, the remarkable architect of the successful surge strategy which helped make all these things possible, is a true American hero.

Where once there was a fighting force of over twelve thousand insurgents, now their numbers have been reduced to approximately one-tenth that size, and they are becoming more and more isolated.

Not all of the victories are military, either. We are also working to win the hearts and minds of the populace, which is, and always has been, an important part of the equation.

General Petraeus and his forces have not only nearly defeated al-Qaeda on the battlefield, they have convinced the local tribal leaders that al-Qaeda is their enemy, too, and that will pay dividends in the war on terror for years to come.

The war is not yet over and there is still much work to be done, but all these things taken together add up to a truly amazing accomplishment, and something all Americans should be proud of.

But few of these things make the front page of our daily newspapers or lead off the nightly newscasts.

Stars and Stripes, the newspaper which has served the United States Armed Forces since it was founded by union troops during the civil war, is delivered under the auspices of MWR.

Our papers were initially printed in Baghdad by Iraqis, and delivered by truck to the Victory Base Complex gate, where MWR staff would meet the Iraqi driver to transfer the papers into smaller vans for delivery to MWR facilities, DFACs, and other military points throughout the area.

The Iraqi drivers would make a practice of disguising their load to avoid attack by insurgents, but one day the driver was killed by sniper fire just before reaching the gate.

For several days we received no deliveries while the Iraqis moved the entire printing operation to Kuwait, and for weeks thereafter, the papers were flown in every day for pick-up at the airport and delivered under armed escort until things outside the wire calmed down enough so that the printing could be resumed in Baghdad.

I wonder what the editors of major newspapers in the United States, who often leave stories such as this off their front pages, would think of such heroic efforts to deliver the news to those who no longer have the luxury of taking such things for granted?

I am still in awe of the brave men and women who not only fight for the rights of the dispossessed to enjoy the things we take for granted, but also fight for the rights of those who would criticize or ignore such efforts.

"Congress shall make no law respecting an establishment of religion, or prohibiting the free exercise thereof; or abridging the freedom of speech, or of the press; or the right of the people peaceably to assemble, and to petition the Government for a redress of grievances." – First Amendment to the U.S. Constitution.

It is easy to forget that billions of people all over the world do not enjoy the freedoms we are guaranteed by that wonderful document.

While the Iraqis must ultimately take control of their own destiny, they have written a constitution under our guidance which suits their citizenry, they have held elections and elected representatives, and they have even held a televised debate between their two candidates during their presidential election.

It is an awesome thing to know that we, as Americans, have helped birth a democracy in the Middle East which will surely make the world a less dangerous place for us all in the future.

35

BREATHLESS

Persecution

Blessed are those who are persecuted because of righteousness,
for theirs is the kingdom of heaven.
Matthew 5:1

"Mommy, don't cry. We can get a new daddy."

I just looked at my youngest son in surprise. Byron was nine years-old and only trying to console his mother, but the shock of those words hit me like a cold slap in the face. I will never forget them.

Those words, as much as anything else, brought home to me the fact that I had been with Bobby for half my life and I wasn't at all sure how to exist in a world without him. But even more, I realized how badly my sons were going to miss their father.

I still felt like a young woman, but suddenly I was a 40 year-old widow with two children. As lost as I felt, my greatest concern was how my sons would fare without their daddy.

I immediately realized I needed as much help as I could get from family and friends.

My husband's business partner in the Idaho gold mine was a long-time family friend and member of our church. He owned numerous other business interests, but was known to everyone as Captain McClintock because of his tugboat business.

We often socialized with him and his wife, even going on vacations together, and I was grateful the Captain immediately stepped in to offer his help and support after Bobby's death. He was a trusted friend, just what I needed at the time.

Little did I know his intentions were less than honorable, even nefarious.

After the funeral, my brother Jerry and another church member went to Idaho to pick up the rest of Bobby's things.

While there, they attempted to speak with Gary, our former tenant whom we'd hired to work the mine, and who had reportedly discovered Bobby's body. He was not at the trailer on the property, but eventually Jerry found him at a tavern in a nearby town with a local woman. I'm sure Gary's wife back in Slidell would have been none-too-pleased. Gary was drunk, and the story he told my brother didn't mesh with the story he had given the funeral director.

He wasn't clear on exactly where he had found Bobby, whether he had carried him from the mine or from the road, and there were other details which changed over time. Even when he sobered up, there was something about his story that never rang true. I was not then, nor have I ever been, satisfied with his testimony.

Gary finally claimed that Bobby had lowered himself by rope into the mine to take samples, and at one point asked him to retrieve some supplies. When he returned, Gary said he found the rope broken and the mine partially caved in.

But the story just didn't mesh with his earlier versions, or with the local sheriff who questioned whether Gary could have retrieved Bobby's body by himself and carried him to the road where he was ultimately found.

Years earlier, just after we were married, Bobby took a trip with my family. We stopped at an abandoned mine in Colorado. My brother Jerry and Bobby just had to explore, so I went along to keep them out of trouble. We crossed a rickety bridge leading to the entrance, and looked around the outside of the mine. After a while it was time to head back. Jerry and I crossed the bridge to return to where my parents were waiting, but when we got to the other side and turned around, Bobby was gone.

For several minutes we shouted for him, to no avail.

Jerry laughed and told me not to worry, that Bobby had obviously gone inside the mine to explore and would soon return, but I was inconsolable. For reasons I could not fully explain, I was convinced Bobby had left me, never to return. I had a full-blown panic attack, crying and furious all at the same time, with the irrational belief I would never see Bobby again.

Well, of course he returned, but not to a warm welcome. I made him promise never to do anything like that again. He did, of course, and was very apologetic, but I've often wondered if that terrible feeling I had when he disappeared was a premonition of what was to come twenty years later.

After hearing the different versions from Gary, I was extremely troubled and confided my feelings to the Captain, who immediately offered to 'look into things.'

He brought Gary back to Slidell and put him to work on one of his tugboats, in order to 'keep an eye on him.' He told me he didn't want Gary to know of our suspicions for the time being.

I was, of course, very upset and just trying to get through each day with my sons, so I was more than willing to trust what the Captain told me.

Imagine my shock when not long after that a process server arrived on my doorstep with legal papers outlining the Captain's request to the court to conserve my children and exercise power-of-attorney over me!

This man had stood up at Bobby's funeral and cried. He had spoken eloquently of their friendship and professed his intention that as long as he lived, neither me, nor my sons, would ever want for anything. And within a month of his moving eulogy I received legal papers I did not fully understand, but appeared to outline his intention to upend our lives even beyond the death of my husband and their father.

I called his office immediately, but his secretary would not allow me to speak with him, so I went to his house. His wife answered the door, and with a pained look, would only tell me to "talk to my husband" before closing the door in my face.

I found out later the Captain had even tried to "jump my claim" on the mine, filing false papers with the local assayer which caused me even more time and expense, not to mention the heartache of painful memories as I undid his dirty deeds.

What hurt the most was not that the Captain had treated me this way, but that Bobby, who in life had trusted and befriended him, counseled and advised him, was betrayed so terribly in death.

Though we lived in the same area for many years after, neither he nor his wife ever spoke to me again.

During this time of legal wrangling, I was in a state of shock, as you might imagine. On top of Bobby's death, it seemed like his trusted friend was attempting to take his children away from their mother.

Of course that wasn't his intent at all. He was actually trying to control the gold mine and my sons' interest as Bobby's heirs.

I was forced to hire an attorney, who was finally able to quash all the demands the Captain had made in his legal filings. It was a very stressful time, but my children were being threatened and I didn't have the luxury of a normal grieving process.

Any mother becomes a formidable adversary when her children are in danger, and I was certainly no exception. I prayed for strength and asked the Lord to protect what was left of my family.

Some time later, I was contacted by another attorney who offered to "get to the bottom of things" with Gary, who remained in the employ of the Captain for years after that terrible experience.

When I asked him what he meant exactly, he made it clear without being too specific that he was willing to use shady methods to get the truth from Gary. I took this to mean he would not stop at physical violence against the man.

I know many would have welcomed such actions, or at least the sense of closure one might think would follow. Many would want revenge on the person whom I now believed had been involved in causing the death of my husband, the father of my children.

I could not allow myself to be such a person.

Yes, I was angry. Of course I wanted the truth. But Bobby was gone, and no suffering, deserved or not, would ever bring him back to me. It would have dishonored his memory to allow his loss to be a catalyst for such un-Christian like feelings.

But I admit it was terribly difficult to forgive such a thing.

It is not for us to judge, nor to punish. God alone judges the sins of humanity, and each of us will one day stand before Him to account for our actions.

To err is human, to forgive divine, and when we can love our enemies and forgive those who sin against us, it brings us closer to God.

Judging others is a sin against God. If we love the Lord, we must submit to His will, in good times and bad. It is sometimes difficult, sometimes joyous, but it is always a comfort to know that whatever happens, He is in control.

When Bobby was finally brought home to me, I remember standing over him and wanting more than anything to just hear his voice one more time, to caress his handsome face one last time.

It was overwhelming, and I reached out to touch his cheek.

The funeral director gently caught my sleeve and shook his head.

His action startled me, and I felt a surge of anger through my tears until I realized his reason.

Bobby's head had been crushed, and the mortician who had so carefully reconstructed his face for the funeral was saving me from further heartache.

I would never again touch the face of my beloved husband.

That realization was one of the most difficult moments of my life.

It would be over a decade, long after I had remarried, before I was able to speak his name without trembling, to hear his name spoken without finding myself short of breath.

In death, as in life, Bobby took my breath away

36

MAKING A DIFFERENCE

God's Calling

To man belong the plans of the heart,
but from the LORD comes the reply of the tongue.
All a man's ways seem innocent to him,
but motives are weighed by the LORD.
Commit to the LORD whatever you do,
and your plans will succeed.
The LORD works out everything for his own ends—
even the wicked for a day of disaster.
The LORD detests all the proud of heart.
Be sure of this: They will not go unpunished.
Through love and faithfulness sin is atoned for;
through the fear of the LORD a man avoids evil.
When a man's ways are pleasing to the LORD,
he makes even his enemies live at peace with him.
Better a little with righteousness
than much gain with injustice.
In his heart a man plans his course,
but the LORD determines his steps.
Proverbs 16:1-9

We all have a purpose, and we can all make a difference in the lives of others.

During much of the time I was in Iraq, I slept in a room that was ten feet wide, fourteen feet long, and about twelve feet away from the gravel road the soldiers traversed on their way to and from missions.

But that was all I needed for the task at hand.

Their proximity was a reminder of my purpose.

As I lay there each night listening to the sounds of the Humvees, tanks, and trucks which rumbled by, and the helicopters overhead, I was in a constant state of prayer for those in harm's way. It gave me an overriding purpose for *each day.*

The Lord provides many avenues by which we can serve Him; sometimes our task will change, as will the method by which we seek to achieve that task.

But God's divine purpose for our lives will never change.

It is to serve Him in whatever capacity He decides.

How amazing it is the Lord provides us the opportunity to do His work.

How amazing it was for me to be part of such an enormous undertaking.

We never know exactly what the Lord has in store for us until we accept the challenge to follow His will. It is a job we must accept without preconditions, without knowing the pay, or the hours, or the duration.

It is a lifelong position.

That may sound onerous, but the benefits package simply cannot be beat.

It is a relationship with our Lord and Savior. It is eternal life.

During the second invasion of Fallujah, I counted ninety rockets launched out of Camp Liberty in a single day, just across that road from my office.

In spite of the headache after listening to all that, I still felt safe and protected. I still felt confident all would be well. My future was set.

You can't find job security like that, nowadays.

On another occasion, Sharon had just left my room and was walking back to her quarters when I heard the sound of a rocket overhead, followed by a loud explosion and the acrid smell of smoke.

I called out to Sharon and ran to her, relieved to find her all right. We rushed to her car, because I thought possibly the MWR facility had been hit and I wanted to check on my staff.

When we arrived at the site, we saw that the rocket had landed in the ground next to the chapel, which stood between the landing and the MWR.

Though some of the windows were broken, the chapel itself was fine and no one in either building was hurt.

Protection was provided by the chapel!

How meaningful that the chapel stood between those people and the danger which threatened them.

There were times when full protective gear was required for weeks at a time. Wearing that heavy helmet and vest was almost like putting on a hat and coat in the wintertime. It became almost as natural, although it was one habit I found very easy to break.

That gear I wore served as a barrier between me and outside dangers, just as the chapel had provided a protective shield during that rocket attack.

Ephesians 6:16 says, "Above all, taking the shield of faith, wherewith ye shall be able to quench all the fiery darts of the wicked."

But the chapel itself was not the protection, nor was the vest and helmet I wore. It was the faith in Him which endowed those protections.

Through all my experiences while in Iraq, it was always my faith which sustained me. With faith, I was secure in the knowledge that my Employer was watching out for my well being, and I was not afraid.

Many times I experienced close calls or heard of similar occurrences from others. There was the man seriously injured just outside my office; there was the bullet which missed me by inches as I sat in my office.

There were no casualties resulting from the attack on Camp Falcon, a miracle not reported in the newspapers but which those of us in Baghdad at the time could clearly recognize as such.

There were so many examples of God's protection which inspired and amazed me on a daily basis in Iraq, and yet, if we only pay attention there are many similar instances to be seen in our daily lives no matter where we are.

It's easy to forget how the Lord protects us every single moment of every single day; living in a war zone is just more readily apparent.

As Christians, we need to be constantly thankful for God's goodness, and for the blanket of protection He provides us. It can so often be taken for granted.

I remember one night when security guards brought to my room a distraught woman whose room had just been destroyed by an incoming rocket. Several had hit inside the camp at a time in the evening when most of the rooms would normally have been occupied, and yet not a single person was hurt.

The guards asked if the woman could stay with me for the night; naturally I welcomed her into my 'home.'

Though she was crying hysterically when she arrived, we prayed together, and soon the Lord calmed her and she was able to sleep in peace that night.

Though she returned to the States shortly thereafter, I received an e-mail from her thanking me and telling of her belief that the Lord had placed us together at that time in that place so that she would receive His peace.

The Lord placed me where He wanted me to be, and because I placed my faith in Him, He allowed me to make a difference in her life.

And I, too, was enriched by the experience.

Many times I was approached by others and asked to pray for them, which was as much a comfort to me as it was to them. We both were blessed by the experience.

Sometimes when a soldier told me it was good to see me, I was struck by how much comfort I received by that simple gesture.

Whatever benefit they felt from me, I received tenfold from them.

We are all part of His plan, and if we are open to His will, everything we do will be a part of the good that He does. Everyone and everything is interconnected, and we can all contribute to the protection He provides.

We must all seek His purpose in our lives.

No matter what our surroundings, or what battles we fight, it all boils down to accepting that divine purpose. He will use us in a myriad of ways if only we will invite Him to do so.

It needn't take a war zone to appreciate His protection and accept His will for our lives.

We simply have to understand what's important, and we can make a real difference in our lives and the lives of others.

And that's how even a single person can have an impact in the world.

The Reverend Peter Marshall, a Presbyterian minister who immigrated from Scotland and eventually served two terms as the Chaplain of the United States Senate, once said, "Give us clear vision, that we may know where to stand and what to stand for – because unless we stand for something, we shall fall for anything."

When we stand up for Jesus, regardless of where we are or what is going on around us, we can make a difference.

37
ETERNAL CONNECTIONS

Love

Love is patient, love is kind. It does not envy, it does not boast, it is not proud. It is not rude, it is not self-seeking, it is not easily angered, it keeps no record of wrongs. Love does not delight in evil but rejoices with the truth. It always protects, always trusts, always hopes, always perseveres
1 Corinthians 13:4-7

When the boys and I moved back to Shreveport after Bobby's death, I was focused on starting things anew and helping them get acclimated to this next phase in their lives.

There was a lot to do, and though I am by nature a nester, and had been married my entire adult life, I just could not imagine ever finding anyone to replace Bobby.

I had always looked at Bobby as my soul-mate, and thought such a person only came along once in a lifetime. That's not to say I believed I would never again marry, but Bobby was an awfully tough act to follow.

But we never know what the Lord has in store for us, and God chose to bless me again with a wonderful man named Bob Chriswell.

Bob lived in Indiana, and was the brother-in-law of Don Kitchell, who had been a member of the UPC church which supported Bobby and me as missionaries in France.

During a casual conversation with his wife, Carolyn, I happened to mention jokingly that she should not hesitate to introduce me to any eligible bachelors she knew.

I was not really expecting a response, and had no idea I was going to say that before the words left my mouth, but she told me that she had actually been thinking of talking to me about her brother.

When Carolyn told me he lived halfway across the country that may have made it seem a little 'safer,' especially if things were awkward. It felt almost like a blind date, and I had not really dated since I was in high school. I simply didn't know what to expect, so the distance seemed a small comfort to ease myself into the reality that I was a single woman in the dating pool once more.

Bob called me that very evening, and I was surprised at how eager I was for adult male conversation. It was as if I had been suppressing so much for so long that the floodgates opened, and we talked late into the night.

We began speaking on the phone almost every day, and I looked forward to those conversations with an anticipation I hadn't felt since Bobby was alive.

I tried not to get my hopes up, but it just felt right when we spoke, and our nightly ritual went on for months. We exchanged pictures, and I often looked at his face as we spoke and imagined he was there with me in person.

He finally made plans to come to Shreveport, and as fate would have it, arrived the same weekend that an old friend of Bobby's, Minister Hardt and his wife, were also visiting.

It was almost as if Bobby had sent a chaperone to make sure I would be properly looked after.

I was very excited to finally meet Bob in person, and I fussed with my appearance like a schoolgirl on the night of her prom. My boys teased me quite a bit about that.

As soon as Bob walked in the door, I knew. We were just so comfortable together after all those hours on the phone that he felt like an old friend the moment I laid eyes on him. We had instant chemistry, as they say.

He reminded me a lot of Bobby. They were both gregarious, the type of person who never met a stranger, and I found real comfort in that. Bob was a big man, a strong man who had worked in a factory for many years, but he was also very gentle, as Bobby had been. And he made me laugh more than I had laughed for such a long time. He made me laugh like Bobby had.

We went to church together that night with the Hardts, and Bob confessed he had not been to a service in several years. I told him how committed I was to the Lord, and at the end of the service he felt inspired to rededicate his life to Jesus Christ, which made for a wonderful revival indeed.

A lovely time was had with the Hardts, but neither of us was sorry when they left us alone for the evening.

As Bob and I sat on the porch and talked into the night, I felt as if Bobby was smiling down on me, laughing at how nervous I'd been earlier and so proud of his sons for their little teasing ways, which always make a father happy for all those silly male reasons we sometimes pretend annoy us, but which never really do.

For the first time in ages, I felt at peace, and I knew without a doubt I was holding hands with my future husband, with the approval of my last.

And God was in control.

38

WHERE HE LEADS ME,
I WILL FOLLOW

Obedience

*It is the LORD your God you must follow, and him you must
revere. Keep his commands and obey him; serve him
and hold fast to him*
Deuteronomy 13:4

I told my boys to come sit with me after supper on a warm spring night in
1982. I was nervous for some reason, though I felt sure they would approve
of my decision. Still, it was one thing to consider and quite another thing
to act, and so as I looked into their sweet faces I couldn't help but feel
butterflies.

My boys had both taken to Bob, who had visited several times over the
course of the past year, and they knew we spoke often on the telephone.
I'm sure they sensed what was happening, and could see the joy he brought
into my life.

Still, it was difficult to tell them Bob and I had decided to marry.

They were both smart and mature for their ages, but I was worried,
regardless. After all they had been through, I wanted more than anything
for them to share my happiness. I wanted them to have a father figure in
their lives again, without feeling as if anyone ever would, or could, replace
their father.

Bobby had been such a huge part of all of our lives.

"Bob and I have been doing a lot of praying, and – "

"Are you getting married?" Byron asked.

I just looked at my youngest son in surprise.

The conversation that followed filled my heart with joy. As much as I wanted my boys to be happy, they wanted only the same for me.

As worried as I had been about how they were affected by the turmoil of the past months, they had the same concerns for me. Of course I knew this, but the reminder of their love and devotion at that moment when I had such news to share was overwhelming.

I simply had to cry, and they put their arms around me and hugged my neck until we all were crying. We cried for Bobby's loss, and we cried tears of joy that we still had each other.

We were a family, and as a family we would welcome Bob into our lives, not as a replacement, but an addition. I felt overwhelmed with so many emotions, so proud of my sons for their protective nature, and so happy that the Lord had brought us through such tragedy intact.

We prayed together that the Lord would bless and keep us, and that He would do the same for Bob Chriswell, soon to be part of our family. We thanked Him for the years we had with Bobby, and for bringing Bob into our lives.

I fell asleep that night with the assurance the Lord had His hand on our union.

Bob and I were married in July of that year, almost two years after Bobby's death.

In spite of my sons' immediate acceptance of Bob and our strong bond, the first year of marriage was very difficult, particularly on holidays and anniversaries. But Bob was patient and kind, never envious of the impact Bobby had had on my life. Bob knew how difficult his death had been for me, and was content to let me heal in my own time.

For the first year after Bobby's death, I had visited his grave every day. I was drawn there, and would let nothing keep me from this ritual. I would sit and talk to Bobby as if he were right there listening, and tell him how I was feeling. We had always been so open with each other that sharing my feelings with him was a hard habit to break.

After many months of this, I became angry during my daily visit for the first time. I was upset that Bobby had risked his life, alone in that mine, when his family was depending on him. When he was alive we had often spoken of death and Bobby's belief that mourning was too often grieving for one's self more often than for the departed. Since we, as Christians, were going to Heaven to be with the Lord, Bobby believed those left behind were really feeling sorry for themselves. He did not condemn it, he just understood it, and used that understanding to minister to those left behind.

Well, Bobby was right, and at that moment I *was* feeling sorry for myself, and for the first time since his death I got mad at Bobby. I told him how wrong it was for him to leave his family, to risk his precious life when we needed him so badly. I wept bitter tears until finally I could weep no more.

At long last, my anguish subsided and I became still. I felt all the tension drain from my body, and I was able to turn loose of those feelings. I was filled with God's peace, and He was allowing me to heal. It was all according to His plan.

Not long after that, I was introduced to another Bobby on the telephone. Bobby Chriswell. The first thing I asked him was if he minded if I called him Bob.

Bob was part of His plan, too.

The move to Indiana was bittersweet. The boys and I were leaving a lot of loved ones and an awful lot of memories. Bren in particular had reason to be upset, seeing as how he would be in a new high school for his senior year, but he never complained at all. I felt so blessed to have two such wonderful sons.

Bob was wonderful with them, always treating Bobby's memory with respect. Whenever we spoke of him, Bob was never jealous or resentful. He encouraged us to keep Bobby in our thoughts and conversations, and that's a big part of why our transition was not more difficult than it was.

Another reason was Bob's daughters from his first marriage. Cindy, 20, and Melanie, 14, were treasures, and though they lived with their mother and step-father, they made a delightful addition to our extended family. I had always wanted a daughter, and instantly I had two wonderful girls in my life, along with my wonderful husband!

Bob doted on them, and I was extraordinarily grateful later when he was able to enjoy his beautiful granddaughter Jessica for seven years prior to his death.

It takes a big man to raise another man's family without once letting pride color his behavior. Bob was such a man. His patience seemed infinite, and my love for him grew each day. I took great comfort in watching him with my sons, and how they grew to love him, too. I could not have asked for a better husband.

There were other adjustments to be made, of course. Cambridge, Indiana was a rural community of a few thousand, quite different for someone who had lived in Paris and enjoyed all the conveniences of city living. Even Shreveport was quite different from the pace of living in such a small town by comparison.

Bob loved his garden and loved gardening even more, and though I tried I was just not very good at it and thus did not enjoy it at all.

As much as I cared for Bob and our new life, probably the thing I least enjoyed, aside from gardening, was the slower pace and lack of having whatever you needed within easy driving distance.

But I was happy. After that difficult first year, I really settled in to my new life and felt like Bob and I would be together for the rest of our lives. But I had felt that way before with Bobby, too, and knew that one never knows what the Lord has planned, so I extracted a promise from Bob.

I wanted to make sure that when he retired, we would move to Shreveport so I could be near my aging parents. Daddy and Lois were getting older, and I knew it was where I wanted to be. During my marriage to Bobby, we had traveled all over the world, and even though I had been happiest when we lived abroad as missionaries, I was determined to eventually go home to Louisiana.

Bob made the promise to me before we were married, and little did we both know the sad circumstances under which he would later fulfill that pledge.

Though they were alike in many ways, being married to Bob was much different than being married to Bobby.

We were both older and wiser, of course, as were my children. There was our location, which was different in many ways, but also by virtue of the fact it didn't change from year to year, or even month to month. We were not in constant motion as I sometimes felt Bobby and I had been, as if we might be blown about like leaves on a windy day at a moment's notice.

Bob was a real homebody. He enjoyed making a comfortable home and staying there. Bobby was an adventurer, always looking for the next challenge. Bob was settled, tethered to the land beneath his feet. Bobby sometimes seemed to float above it.

While I loved Bobby, being with Bob was a change for which I was ready. I wanted to nest, and make a home, and Bob took charge of that. I felt very safe and secure with him and the home we had made.

On our first date, I had made clear to Bob my devotion to Christ and His importance in my life. Implicit in that was my hope and expectation he would share my passion. I knew I could never be with a man who didn't love God. When he rededicated his life to the Lord that very night, I could not have been happier.

Yet, when we were married, I confessed to Bob that I was relieved he was not a preacher. I loved the Lord, and wanted to serve Him in all things, but at that point in my life I wanted to go to church and serve Him as just another member of the congregation, and not the preacher's wife.

But four years later, I was reminded once more how God surprises us.

The Lord called Bob to preach.

We had been active in the church and community and were 'nesting' to my heart's content. I was even getting used to the slower pace of the community, and I looked forward to a long, tranquil marriage, watching my sons grow up and start families of their own. I was still no gardener, but Bob was wonderful at it and I had to admit the fresh vegetables were a delightful addition at mealtimes.

Some time prior to my out-of-body experience after my car accident in 1986, Bob came home from work and told me he had a confession to make.

I could tell he was feeling trepidations at the thought of my reaction to what he was about to say, and as you can imagine, my mind was racing. What on earth could my wonderful husband have done which required such a serious prelude, let alone a confession?

He took a deep breath, obviously thinking how I'd told him I hadn't wanted to marry a preacher again, and finally got the words out.

"The Lord's called me to preach."

Well, you can imagine my emotions. What a thing to 'confess.'

I hugged him tightly and didn't say a word for several moments. I was relieved his news was not something bad, I was proud of him for answering the call, and I wanted to compose myself before I spoke. It was a lot to take in and I knew how hard it must have been for him to tell me. But I must admit I felt some resistance.

When we finally parted, all I could say was, "Praise the Lord."

The relief on his face was almost comical, and we collapsed again into each other's arms, laughing and crying all at once.

We prayed together that night as we had never prayed before. I wanted to be supportive, but I also wanted to be anchored after all the years of roaming, especially after the trauma of losing Bobby. I really had not wanted to be married to a preacher again.

Ultimately I had to recognize this was God's path for him. I suppose deep down I was probably afraid of losing him as I had lost Bobby, but I knew I could not deny his calling. Through prayer and with Bob's patience, I accepted his decision.

As supportive as I was, I couldn't help but wonder:

Would Bob measure up to Bobby as a preacher? Would Bob somehow compare himself to my first husband?

It didn't matter to me, of course, but I knew it might cross his mind and I didn't want him to be troubled by it. Bob had actually seen Bobby speak at a church in Indiana years before, and had been quite impressed. Still, Bob had been so wonderful about honoring Bobby's memory, it was probably a silly thing to worry about.

I would soon see that Bob was a wonderful preacher in his own right, though their styles were quite different. Where Bobby was fiery, Bob was deliberate. Bobby was dynamic, but Bob was reassuring. Bob was calm in the pulpit, always measured and steady, while Bobby was on a spiritual tightrope, always unpredictable. But they both loved God and won many souls for the Lord. All glory to His name!

I loved watching Bob develop as a preacher, just as I had with Bobby. Sometimes it brought tears to my eyes to think of how much the Lord had blessed me with two men who loved Him so. I felt so fortunate to have seen and done the things in my life to that point, and it almost felt like the Lord had decided this was the culmination of it all.

But not long after Bob's decision to preach, I survived that terrible car crash and the Lord revealed He was not finished with me, yet. And obviously, He was not finished with Bob, either.

He retired from the factory and devoted himself to study, taking correspondence courses from the United Pentecostal Church while helping me recover from my injuries.

Bob's mother shared with me how she thought he had been called to preach as a teenager, but resisted. We both gave praise at the wonderful ways in which He works.

I often think back to the day I adamantly told Bob I could never be with a man who didn't serve the Lord. And yet not long after, I told him I didn't want to marry a preacher.

How could I have not seen the incongruity of my desires?

There is a French expression, "Le couer a ses raisons, que la raison ne connais pas." It translates, "the heart has its reasons, which reason knows nothing of."

As human beings we are bundles of doubt, fear, and contradictions.

But when we give ourselves over to the Lord, and follow Him wherever He leads us, we will be fulfilled and happy. Sometimes it just takes us a while to realize it.

I didn't want to marry a preacher, and yet that is exactly where the Lord led me. He even used me to bring Bob closer to God, and therefore to the place the Lord wanted him to be: Preaching the Gospel to a new congregation in Cambridge City, Indiana.

The Lord does work in mysterious ways.

"For as many as are led by the Spirit of God, they are the sons of God." - Romans 8:14.

That scripture was the inspiration for one of my favorite hymns, "Where He Leads Me, I Will Follow" by E.W. Blandy, a Salvation Army officer who left a comfortable job in an established church to work along the waterfront slums of New York City over a century ago.

Just another example of God's infinite wisdom and why we must follow wherever He leads us.

Bob and I were right where the Lord wanted us to be.

39

THE LONG GOODBYE

Sickness

Do you not know?
Have you not heard?
The LORD is the everlasting God,
the Creator of the ends of the earth.
He will not grow tired or weary,
and his understanding no one can fathom.
He gives strength to the weary
and increases the power of the weak.
Even youths grow tired and weary,
and young men stumble and fall;
but those who hope in the LORD
will renew their strength.
They will soar on wings like eagles;
they will run and not grow weary,
they will walk and not be faint.
Isaiah 40:28-31

When Bob was diagnosed with prostate cancer, it was quite a blow. We had been married for ten years, and they were filled with happiness. I had finally put down roots and watched my sons grow into fine young men. I had seen Bob become a wonderful preacher in his middle age, having finally answered God's call and found His path, and I had finally gotten over the death of my first husband and found a similarly wonderful man with whom I could spend the rest of my life.

For the first time in my life, I asked God, "Why me?"

Even after Bobby's death, I never dared ask God such a question.

But now I did.

"Why is this happening? What am I supposed to be learning? Why didn't I learn it the first time, with Bobby?"

Naturally I kept these feelings from Bob. I would never have burdened him with such thoughts. But I sought out a dear friend, a wise minister by the name of Ed McFarland.

I asked the same questions of him.

Ed took me firmly by the shoulders.

"Evelyn, this is not to teach you a lesson, this is life!"

His words rang true and I felt as if a heavy burden had been lifted from my shoulders. I know I had learned much from Bobby's death, and from my life experiences, but those words he spoke allowed me to grieve without guilt.

I understood then that the question we need to ask ourselves in times like these is not "Why is this happening to me?" but "How will I react? What would the Lord have me do now?"

Bob battled for four years. There were many, many trips to see specialists at Indiana University Hospital in Indianapolis and MD Anderson Cancer Center in Houston, but ultimately we were told there was nothing more to be done.

True to his word, Bob retired from preaching and brought me home to Shreveport to be close to my parents. He insisted on honoring his promise, and we moved back to Louisiana in late 1995. We were hoping he would have at least another year.

During that time, he suffered terribly but never complained. He always offered kind words to those who visited, and provided comfort to those who knew not how to comfort him.

One of the greatest tributes to Bob was the fact that a good friend of his from Indiana actually moved to Louisiana with his wife to be close to Bob during his last days.

Paul Hopwood was a Presbyterian minister in Cambridge City with whom Bob had developed a close friendship through a ministerial association.

Paul was a dear friend, and had even adjusted the time of his Sunday morning worship service so that I could play the organ there, after which I would rush over to the Methodist service to play the piano, all before returning to our Pentecostal Church to play the piano and complete my Sunday morning marathon.

Paul was near retirement, and moved to Shreveport with his wife, Jane, both of whom were a real comfort to Bob and I. Paul even shaved his head when Bob lost his hair to the cancer treatments. During that difficult year, they were two of many upon whom we relied for support and solace.

My friend Sharon, whom years later I would follow to Baghdad, was also a blessing during this time. She was always available to assist with Bob or just to lend an ear if I was feeling especially overwhelmed.

My son, Bren, was living in Idaho, so Byron and his wife, Stephanie also moved from Indiana to be with us in Louisiana. Byron was only nine when his father died, and had grown especially close to Bob, whom he called Pop. He truly loved Pop as if he was his own father, and his wife quickly agreed to come with him to Shreveport. Stephanie reminded me of Naomi and Ruth in the Bible. She loved us enough to leave her own family to care for us.

I had hospice care for Bob during the day when I had to work, and I cared for him at night. We shared many beautiful conversations, and though it was difficult for us both, I treasure the time we spent together during those long nights.

Bob was hospitalized a week prior to his death. I stayed with him the entire time. Even in his last days, he found the strength to sing the Ricky Skaggs song "I Wouldn't Change You if I Could," and I would melt just as I always had. His voice was weaker now, but his eyes still twinkled like they had when we were first married. Whenever I hear that song today,

I'm not sad, but filled with happy memories of Bob and our wonderful life together.

All those who came to see him during those last days were amazed by his attitude. I watched Bob lay a hand on the shoulders of grown men as they wept, kneeling at his bedside. I was overwhelmed by his compassion and strong desire that all those who came to comfort be comforted themselves. The Spirit of the Lord was present in that room, and all who entered were blessed in His name.

When Bob finally labored to take his last, slow breaths, I held his hand, told him I loved him, and that it was all right to go. Moments later, he died.

His long struggle was finally over.

I walked into the hall, where family and friends were waiting, and told them Bob was gone. After their final goodbyes, everyone began to leave except for Byron.

"I'm going back in for Pop," he told me.

"No, Byron. The nurses need to prepare him."

The nurses had told me they would get Bob ready for pickup by the funeral home, which had already been notified.

Byron took me by the shoulders, tears streaming down his face, and said, "You don't understand. I couldn't be there for Dad when he died. I need to be there for Pop."

So Byron washed and prepared Bob for the arrival of the funeral home personnel, like the good son that he was.

I have never been more proud.

40

GUARDIAN ANGELS

Spiritual Intervention

Are not all angels ministering spirits sent to serve those
who will inherit salvation?
Hebrews 1:14

When we returned home that night, we were met at the door by our dog, Bear. She had lain beside Bob's bed during his entire illness. Byron knelt down and hugged her, and she began to cry.

Byron rubbed her back when suddenly she broke from his embrace and ran into the bedroom where she had spent so many hours at Bob's bedside. We could hear her moving around the room, whimpering and crying.

As we followed her in, we passed the grandfather clock in the hall, which had stopped at the exact time of Bob's death. We all noticed it at the same moment, and just stared in silence.

None of us had ever known the clock to stop.

Years before, shortly after Bob was first diagnosed with cancer, Bear had a litter of puppies. Bob fixed up a wooden crate with blankets in the garage for her and the pups.

Late that night, the phone rang in our bedroom. I answered quickly, so as not to wake up Bob, who had finally drifted off to sleep.

I heard a man's voice ask for Bob Chriswell. I told him that Bob was asleep, and asked him if I could help. It was well past midnight, and I didn't want to disturb him if I didn't have to.

"I saw your Chow on the road over from your house, and since I've never seen her out of your yard, I thought you should know."

"I don't see how," I responded. "Bear just had puppies and she's with them in our garage."

"No," he said, "I'm sure it was your dog."

We had the same exchange again, and the man was adamant that we should check our garage to make sure. Finally, I woke up Bob and put him on the phone, thinking he might know the man.

I heard basically the same conversation until finally Bob said, "Hold on, I'll check." He got out of bed and made his way downstairs.

When he opened the door to the garage, to his surprise Bear and the puppies, whose eyes were not yet open, were huddled at the crack under the door to get air. The garage was filled with smoke, and suddenly their bed and the crate burst into flames.

I had followed Bob, and hurriedly began filling buckets of water in the laundry room to help him extinguish the fire. There were several cans filled with gas for the snowmobile and lawn mower near the dogs' bed, all of which would have combusted quickly had Bob not gone down to the garage when he did.

When things were finally under control, we went back upstairs, having forgotten entirely about the strange phone call until we noticed the receiver still off the hook.

The man had hung up.

Bear was a red chow, unusual for the area, so we drove around the country roads for several evenings, looking for a dog that might have been mistaken for Bear, but found none. We even placed an ad looking for the person who had phoned us at that time and in those circumstances, but no one ever called. Previously, when we wanted to mate Bear, we had placed an ad looking for a red chow, but found none then, either.

When Bear reacted as she did after Bob's death, I remembered that unusual event, and how that strange voice had insisted we check our garage, saving our lives in the process.

Was that our guardian angel, acting because God was not finished with us yet?

I know there are many who would be skeptical, who don't believe God sends angels to watch over us. Those people would ascribe such events to coincidence, or chance. Even some Christians may find these things hard to believe.

But with faith, anything is possible.

And God is always in control.

Whose voice was really on the other end of that phone call?

Where was the dog that looked like Bear?

Did such a dog really exist?

Hebrews 1:14 says, "Are not all angels ministering spirits sent to serve those who will inherit salvation?"

I believe in guardian angels!

41
WINDS OF CHANGE

Commitment

Do not love the world or anything in the world. If anyone loves the world, the love of the Father is not in him. For everything in the world—the cravings of sinful man, the lust of his eyes and the boasting of what he has and does—comes not from the Father but from the world. The world and its desires pass away, but the man who does the will of God lives forever.
1 John 2:15-17

A shamal is a strong wind which blows across the lower valley of the Tigris and Euphrates rivers, often arriving suddenly and causing destructive, blinding sandstorms. Arabs have always been fascinated by the winds because, for Bedouin tribes, such drastic weather changes can mean the difference between life and death.

The first major shamal usually occurs around the end of May, followed by an even more violent storm period in early June. During this period, fishermen often remain in port, believing the winds will actually devour their crafts.

I was actually in Baghdad during one of the most notable shamals in recent history, in the summer of 2005. Over a thousand people were treated for respiratory problems, and the entire city came to a standstill.

These winds are also called Barih, which translates in Arabic as 'calamity.'

As the millennium approached, such an ill wind was blowing my way.

I met Barry in the summer of 1999. Or, I should say, became reacquainted with him. Barry and his wife had been members of the church where I attended in the early 1960's, and had a son who had been best friends with Byron growing up.

Unfortunately, in the intervening years, Barry and his wife had gotten divorced.

Unfortunate in more ways than one.

Bob had been gone for three years and I honestly was still somewhat out of sorts. I still felt a little unsettled, unsure of things. After years of globe-trotting with Bobby and our dynamic lifestyle, I had become very serene in my life with Bob. He was the perfect partner at that point in my life, when I craved stability.

I dearly loved Bobby, but Bob brought a sense of calm to my life I desperately needed after my adventurous first marriage.

I felt safe and secure with Bob, but now, once again, I had lost my husband and found myself without a partner. Of course, with God one is never alone.

Though my friends and family were quite dear to me and a solid means of support, I missed the daily companionship and intimacy that only comes from a loving spouse. After all, I had married at eighteen and only been without a partner for about two of the next thirty years or so.

I knew from experience that I had to keep busy, but I also needed the extra income to support myself, so I took a job at an agency in Shreveport, working with teen-age mothers to assist them with developing their parenting skills. It could be difficult work, but it was always rewarding, and I threw myself into it with all my energies.

I made new friends there, some wonderful co-workers who further expanded my social support system and helped me stay busy, but there was a definite void in my life that had been filled so long by the two men I had loved and married.

After Bobby's death, I was only forty and felt much too young to be widowed. Though I was devastated by his loss, in the back of my mind I always believed I would marry again. While I didn't know what the future held, I felt that the Lord would lead me again to someone with whom I could share myself.

Then God brought Bob into my life.

But after Bob died, I wasn't so sure about things. I was nearing sixty, and it seemed like a very real possibility to me that my married years might be over. I was at an age when almost everyone I knew was married, and I still felt too young to be a widow. But since almost all of my peers were married, I wondered whether I would find anyone else, and even whether that was truly what I wanted.

Marriage had always been my 'natural state,' but I found myself increasingly curious as to what my life might be like without a partner after all those years.

Plus, I had doubts about finding someone else who would measure up to the two wonderful men with whom the Lord had blessed me.

Both Bobby and Bob were awfully tough acts to follow.

So I slowly began to move on with my life, filling my hours with worship, family, and friends. I had my job, which was fulfilling in many ways. I had always enjoyed helping others, and it was gratifying to work with young mothers who were at such an important stage in their development, a time from which I was far removed but could remember as if it were yesterday.

But though I began to settle into a new phase of my life once more, I still wondered if there might be big changes in store for me. I had learned from so many events in my life over the years that nothing should be taken for granted, and God always has a path for us. I did not believe He was through with me yet, and I was eager for whatever He placed before me. And as much as I had enjoyed sharing my life with the men I loved, I was resigned to the fact that the Lord may have other plans.

I decided that if the Lord would have me continue my journey without a partner, I was okay with that. I was ready for whatever came next. Praise God from who all blessings flow!

I am not, and have never been, a shrinking violet. In spite of being ready for a more sedate life after Bobby's death, I have never been afraid to try new things. I always embrace a challenge, and I enjoy this wonderful life God has given me to the fullest.

I learned to ski in Germany at the age of twenty-one and I learned to snowboard in my sixties!

One of the things I have always been amused by is the perception among some non-Christians that fun and faith are somehow contradictory. Nothing could be further from the truth. Being a Christian is fun! It is joyous! Life is a precious gift from God, and He wants us to enjoy it. Even some Christians need to be reminded of that on occasion.

But that doesn't mean things will always be easy, or enjoyable. In all our lives will be pain and disappointment. If we never traveled through the deepest valley, how could we truly appreciate the highest mountaintop?

What happened next was another valley. But it led me to the highest mountain.

As someone who lost a husband to both a sudden accident and to a long, lingering illness, I have often thought about which of those experiences was the more painful to endure.

Some might believe that the sudden loss would be easier, akin to ripping the bandage off quickly, with no time to prepare or think. Others might say the latter is preferable, because there is time to prepare for the tragedy, as painful as that will be.

I've come to believe losing Bobby was the most difficult for me.

They were both terrible experiences, of course, and neither was easy.

I loved Bob deeply and completely, and he was a wonderful husband and partner. And while it was so very hard to lose him to cancer, we were able to spend many wonderful hours together, time we used to say all the things that need to be said to those we love. It was a great comfort to have the opportunity to tell him goodbye, something Bobby's sudden death did not afford.

And of course, Bobby was my first love, and there's nothing quite like that.

I had many wonderful years with Bobby when we were both so young and adventurous, followed by many peaceful years with Bob in middle age. I was so incredibly grateful to the Lord for these two men, and I know I would have been content had I lived the rest of my years alone.

Both men were mountaintops, and losing them were the two lowest valleys of my life. I say this because while what happened next was terrible for me to go through, it simply cannot compare to the loss of either of my husbands.

What happened was Barry.

Barry, a doctor, had been divorced for several years, so when we ran into each other one day, we had both been alone for long enough to miss the comforts which come with married life.

Barry was different from Bob, a little less open but still friendly and solicitous. We struck up a friendship, speaking frequently on the telephone and having dinner together after work. The fact we had first met in church was comforting to me, although I must admit that I was a little bothered that he was divorced.

Still, I didn't pass judgment on that point; I understood that not everyone was as blessed as I had been. To this day I know many fine people whose marriages have ended in divorce, and unless we have led perfect lives we cannot judge.

Barry and I hit it off right away. We were close in age, from the same area, and seemingly eager for good, old-fashioned adult conversation.

We talked about our lives and our spouses, and it was like a dam broke for me. I was actually a little surprised I felt the need for companionship again so strongly. Just when I had begun to believe I might never remarry, here was a man who seemed to have that very idea in his head, and rather quickly at that.

I am a decisive person, and I have always been attracted to people who know what they want and are firm in their goals.

So I was not surprised when he asked me to marry him. I could see that he was interested in me and knew it was coming. At the time, I felt like we were compatible and would be comfortable in a relationship together.

I didn't realize at the time, of course, but I had completely misjudged him and his intentions. That fact only added to my pain and humiliation later.

Still, it seemed like it could work, and we began to talk seriously about marriage.

Barry and I were also both at the stage in life when directness comes more and more easily, so I was very frank with him right away.

If I were to ever marry again, I would have to be certain of two things: As I had told Bob, I could never share myself with a man who did not love the Lord. And at this point in my life, I also needed to be certain that my husband could support me financially.

Of course, I always wanted financial security before, but now it was more of a factor than it had been in the past due to my particular situation. During this time, I relied not only on my employment for income, but on two pensions I received based on my husbands' work during our marriages.

According to the rules governing the larger of the two pensions, if I remarried I would lose that monthly payment. That pension, which I would continue to receive as long as I lived if I remained unmarried, would vanish forever once I took another husband.

The remaining pension was quite small and not nearly enough to support me even with my work income, so the decision to remarry was a very serious one for me.

Barry acted very understanding, and promised me that he would support me and take care of the income I would lose as a result of our union.

"You will never want for anything," he said.

I didn't make the connection at the time, but those were almost the exact words the Captain had told me after Bobby's death.

We discussed many other issues, of course, and ultimately I decided to accept his proposal. Barry and I were married in the fall of 1999.

It was one of the biggest mistakes of my life.

At first, everything was fine. We loved each other, or so I thought, but I still recognized this was definitely a different type of love than what I'd previously experienced.

But I had also felt my love for Bob was slightly different than what I'd shared with Bobby, so I simply trusted that things would be fine. I really did care for Barry, and honestly believed he cared for me, too. I could never have married him, otherwise.

A couple of my female friends expressed reservations about him, warning me in slightly oblique ways not to rush into things, but I was in love and felt lucky to have found someone to spend my life with once more. I suppose I discounted their opinions.

One might look back and wish they had made other decisions, but even though I went through much unpleasantness with Barry, I came out on the other side right where the Lord wanted me to be. I give praise to God for everything which followed, even though it was difficult to endure at the time. I am living proof the Lord truly does work in mysterious ways!

As I said, everything seemed fine initially. But a few months into our marriage, I began to notice a different side to him. At first it was just little things, and I may have chalked it up to the 'getting to know' him period, as married couples understand. But it eventually became alarming to me.

Barry was secretive about certain things, something I had not experienced with either Bob or Bobby. They had both been so open and giving in marriage, and I was used to sharing everything with my husband, and having everything shared with me in return. More and more I was beginning to realize how very blessed I had been in my previous relationships, but I told myself that very few men were like either Bobby or Bob, and I tried to give my new husband the benefit of the doubt.

Just as I had not wanted Bob to feel like he needed to 'measure up' to Bobby, I attempted to refrain from making unfavorable comparisons in my mind, but it became increasingly difficult as time went on.

Before we married, Barry and I had our attorneys draw up agreements which would protect the assets which we both brought into the marriage. I had signed his documents right away and given him copies, but Barry kept putting me off with his signature on my documents. Either his attorney was still looking over the papers or he had left them at his office. It was always something.

This was not a major concern at first, and certainly not something I even thought about every day. Every now and then I would remember and remind him, but it seemed as though he always had an excuse.

Barry would tell me not to worry, he'd 'take care of it' soon, and I really wanted to trust him. When you love someone, you want to believe the best of them.

But soon enough, there were other things which started to bother me, as well.

I had been doing the bookkeeping, preparing information for Barry's accountant to use on our tax return. Barry owned a large farm where he kept and raised cattle, and I noticed some irregularities in expenses assigned between his practice and the farm.

Because Barry had insisted we file jointly, I was concerned about any problems with our tax return. I knew very well that I was responsible for anything above my signature, and I wanted to know exactly what I was signing.

I mentioned to Barry that some of the figures didn't seem to add up, but his response was much like our other paperwork. He told me he'd take care of things.

"Trust me," he'd say.

But now I was really having my doubts.

Barry continued to insist I sign the tax return, until one night I finally had to insist to him in no uncertain terms that I would absolutely not sign unless he fully explained the discrepancies I had found and accounted for all the amounts on the joint return. I simply would not sign a fraudulent or inaccurate tax return.

At this point, the real Barry came out, and I was completely unprepared.

He stormed out of the house, enraged.

I was stunned at his reaction. I really didn't know what to think, but his actions obviously concerned me. Aside from the fact that I had married a man who now seemed the opposite of the person I had promised to love and cherish, I had also given up a lot financially. Barry's behavior toward me was growing increasingly erratic and suspicious.

I was beside myself as to what to do next. I felt sad, worried, and frightened all at the same time.

The next morning Barry again requested I sign the tax form, this time nicely, as if the incident the night before had never occurred. So I asked him again if he would please bring me the information for which I'd been asking, which he had assured me would allay my suspicions about the return. He looked me straight in the eye and promised me he would that very evening.

So I signed the return.

As he left the house that morning, I stopped him at the door and kissed him, saying, "I don't know why, but it still feels like you're keeping something from me."

His eyes grew as wide as saucers, and for a moment he froze like a deer caught in the headlights. Although I had no idea what would take place later that day, my heart sank at the look in his eyes.

Finally he said, "I've got to go," and rushed out the door.

Those were the last civil words he ever spoke to me.

When I returned home a little earlier than usual that afternoon, I was surprised to find movers parked in front of my house. Since Barry's first wife had remained in their house after his divorce, he had moved in with me after we were married.

I got out of my car and watched in shock as movers rolled furniture out the front door and toward their truck. I told them to stop and rushed into the house, meeting Barry, who was obviously on his way out.

"What on earth is going on?" I asked him.

He barely looked up and walked right past me and out the door.

I was stunned. Every moment was more bizarre than the next. It looked like half of my things had already been loaded onto the truck. I hurried out the door after him.

"Barry, wait a minute!"

But he was already getting into his car.

I ran over, and when he stopped the car at the end of the driveway before turning onto the street, I jumped into the passenger seat.

For the first time that day he really looked at me, and I believe he was now as surprised by me as I had been by him.

"Barry, please stop this and tell me what is going on."

But he wouldn't. I begged him to just come back with me to the house and talk, but he absolutely refused. He would not even move the car until I got out.

Finally, I did and walked back to the house as he sped off down the street. There was really nothing more I could do.

I did manage to stop the movers and get them to unload my things, but that was small comfort. I had never been treated like that in my entire life. It was surreal, coming home to find my husband behaving in such a way. In spite of the tax return, and the pre-nuptial agreements, I was still totally blind-sided by what had happened.

My pastor, Michael Hudspeth, and his wife, Glenda, who had been with me through the difficult times after the death of both my previous husbands, graciously came over that evening and spent several hours with me, along with my brother Verdell and his wife Galyn, and my son Byron. Bren was in Idaho, but prayed with me over the telephone.

I can't begin to convey what the love and support from these friends and family members meant to me during those dark hours. The Spirit was with us that night in my home, and in spite of everything I sang the Lord's praises and blessed His name for all He had provided.

The Lord will never ask us to accept a burden greater than we can bear.

At the end of the day, after the movers had finally gone and I had spent hours in prayer and conversation with my loved ones, I collapsed into bed. I was physically and emotionally drained, but it was still difficult to go to sleep.

I was completely exhausted.

But finally, the Lord provided the rest I sorely needed, as I knew He would.

"Come unto Me all ye that labor and are heavy laden, and I will give you rest." – Matthew 11:28.

Come unto Me.

What comforting words!

God uses trials and tribulations to remind us to lay our burdens at His feet, and come unto Him. Just as a parent will sense when something is wrong with a child, the Lord knows our hearts and is eager to bless us in times of trouble.

As I finally drifted off to sleep, I couldn't get over the odd events of that day.

But that was just the beginning of the strange saga of my third marriage.

The next day I was served with divorce papers, which had obviously been prepared in advance of the previous day's events. What was going on? What was he trying to accomplish? The questions rolled through my head until I got to one with implications which made me spring into action.

What else was he planning?

I immediately took the divorce papers to my lawyer, who did some checking and soon discovered what else Barry had done, and things became much clearer.

Barry had taken out a loan against my house, which I had owned free and clear, to satisfy a settlement with his ex-wife. And that was only the beginning of the problems he had caused me.

I felt sick to my stomach. To think of what I had given up, in order to marry this man, and all that I had sacrificed because I trusted him.

I felt humiliated. It was embarrassing to have been so foolish, to be taken in by this person. How could I have trusted him? Why was he doing this to me?

But as soon as that thought entered my head, I stopped.

I remembered the conversation with Ed McFarland after Bob was diagnosed with cancer. This was not some punishment, "it was life", he had said. And the test for me as a Christian was, how will I react to this trial? It's easy to be steadfast when things are going well. But the real test of faith is in how we deal with adversity.

I prayed for strength and began to act. I told my attorney we needed to make sure my house was safe, and file a response to the divorce papers with the court.

Barry and I were legally separated in April of 2001. We had been married for less than a year-and-a-half.

For the next several months, I worked to disentangle this man from my life, which seemed like a full time job. I later discovered that he had even forged my signature on a large tax return check made out to both of us. He'd even thought ahead and changed the return address to his office to complete the subterfuge.

Half of the refund was rightfully mine, and I desperately needed the money, but ultimately I dropped the matter. An F.B.I. agent told me I could have him arrested, but I did not want to embarrass his family or harm his medical practice.

By the time of our divorce proceedings, I just wanted to be rid of him. I had been struggling with my self-confidence, ashamed I had allowed myself into such a position, and I knew the best thing for me was to move on as quickly as I could.

It was an arduous process, but I managed to get a portion of the funds from the loan repaid, though not all. My attorney also discovered the pre-nuptial agreement had never been filed as Barry told me, which explained why he had never provided a copy for my attorney. Without that document being filed with the court, the judge could not order Barry to pay me what he'd promised to pay to replace my pension, which was now gone.

In the blink of an eye my financial state was in shambles, and I was very worried about what to do. I continued working, but my salary plus the smaller pension payment did not begin to cover my monthly bills. My savings would soon be depleted unless I did something.

In September of that year, when two planes hit the World Trade Center in New York City, like all Americans and others around the world, I was horrified.

When something like that happens, it's hard to feel sorry for oneself in light of others experiencing suffering of such magnitude. Just as that event was a wake-up call for our entire nation, it also reminded me how blessed my life had been.

At our divorce proceedings in November, my lawyer made a vigorous argument on my behalf. After looking over the evidence, the judge then called a very unusual meeting in his chambers.

An ex parte hearing is when the judge meets with one party outside the presence of the opposing party. Only my attorney and I were present.

"When we go back into court, I'm going to ask you to do something I've never before counseled anyone to do in my entire career," the judge told me.

I looked at my attorney, who just nodded. Puzzled, I turned back to the judge, and I could hardly believe my ears.

The judge told me to lie.

Apparently, he and my attorney had come to the conclusion that I had been treated so egregiously, and my options were so bleak, that they were advising me to commit perjury to make things right.

If I lied in open court, I could get my pension back.

The nightmare of my third marriage would become but a bad memory, and once more I would be able to support myself and keep a roof over my head.

One little lie. Under oath.

But was that really all there was to it?

Matthew 19:6 says, "Wherefore they are no more twain, but one flesh. What therefore God hath joined together, let not man put asunder."

Like it or not, Barry and I had been joined together in the eyes of God, by a servant of God, in the house of God. And that was a sacred thing to me, as it is for any Christian.

While I had no control over Barry's actions when he filed those divorce papers, I was responsible for what I did, and denying my vows would be the same to me as denying my faith, and that I could not do.

How could I place my hand on God's Holy Book and swear that my marriage had not been consummated, no matter what the financial reward?

I looked into the kind eyes of the judge, and answered, "No."

Both he and my attorney strenuously urged me to reconsider.

"It's the only way," they pleaded, "otherwise you'll lose everything."

But I couldn't do it, though I knew it would help me tremendously. There would be no earthly consequence because the judge would shield me from any such punishment.

No one would ever know.

Except for me.

And God.

Our actions when no one is watching are every bit as important as those we show the world, because He is always with us.

Matthew 16:26 teaches, "For what will it profit a man if he gains the whole world, and loses his soul?"

As I turned this over in my mind, I knew what I had to do.

I told the truth and lost the pension. My lawyer was angry, my sons were angry, even the judge was upset. But the best course is always the right course, and it's usually pretty easy to figure out what that is. All we have to do is take it.

I walked out of the courtroom a poorer woman financially but a richer one for God's wisdom. I understood the judge only wanted to help me, but I had to answer to a higher authority.

My son Bren, his wife Traci and their children moved in with me to help with expenses, but it was clear I would have to find a way to climb out of the deep hole in which Barry's deceit had left me.

So I turned to the Lord in prayer.

I've always believed that whenever things are at their lowest, we must look to the Lord and trust Him to show us the way. If we believe on Him, and truly accept that He is in control, He will not let us down.

Though it may not be the response we want, He will answer our prayers. Though it may not be the path we would choose, He will show us the way. And if we trust in Him, He will lead us to a cause more important than ourselves.

This was how the Lord brought me to Iraq.

Going there would help ease the financial burden with which Barry had left me, while putting me in a blessed place to serve His name. How perfect was that?

God showed me in many different ways the road He had chosen for me. It was up to me to trust in Him and accept it. He spoke to me through Sharon. He even spoke to me through Barry.

And He spoke to me through the judge, whose well-intentioned but ultimately untenable plan taught me an important lesson.

This is why I live my life with no regrets, because I trust the Lord to put me right where He wants me to be. I don't look backwards, but focus instead on the road ahead so I can stay on the path He's chosen for me.

My marriage to Barry ended up serving the will of God.

"And we know that all things work together for good to them that love God, to them who are the called according to his purpose." – Romans 8:28.

Not long after my divorce, I arrived in Iraq.

Once again, I felt God's perfect peace, and knew without a doubt that He was in control.

42

PILGRIMAGE

Following

Blessed is the man whose strength is in You.
Whose heart is set on pilgrimage.
Psalm 84:5

"There are many things about tomorrow

    I don't seem to understand,

    But I know who holds tomorrow

    And I know who holds my hand."

- Ira F. Stamphill

If I were to draw a map of my life for those who came after me to follow, it would wind its way across forty-nine states and almost as many countries, but it would never veer very far from home.

Its route would travel along many of the smaller roads, those spurs which branch off the beaten path, and wend its way back and forth across the softened folds like the tide gently lapping against the shore.

Every crease would tell a story, every story would teach a lesson, and every lesson would lead to yet another experience, another crease, and the journey would begin again.

But the crux of my journey, my pilgrimage, my map, would always begin and end with Jesus Christ. In all of my travels, the one constant has been my relationship with the Lord.

The map of my life would mirror my heart, filled with the hard-won wisdom and experience which defies expectations and surprises the traveler at every turn.

And yet when the map is examined, each path would seem to be the only path, every twist and turn would follow a natural progression.

In hindsight, each byway would appear the logical choice.

But when the map was finally and completely unfolded, one would see that the last panel is blank.

My map, not yet complete; my life, a work-in-progress.

The Lord is not finished with me, yet.

I believe I still have many miles to go, many places to explore, many exciting things to do before I reach my final destination.

God has always been right there with me, traveling beside me, watching over me, and protecting me as I journey onward.

Whenever I needed a little push, He was there.

If I required a wake-up call, He provided it.

And when I had to be carried, He lifted me up and placed me right where He wanted me to be.

Throughout my life, that is what I strived for.

I did not always achieve what He asked of me. Many, many times I fell short of His expectations, but each time He forgave me, and allowed me to continue.

Following God can be scary because He does not always reveal His destination. He will often lead us from the familiar to the unknown. But He will also give us the peace of mind to follow, and great blessings await those who persevere in His name.

With God, I am unafraid of a future I cannot see.

With Him, all things are possible.

So many wonderful people I've known, so many wonderful people yet to meet.

Life is full of beautiful things, and it's important for us to realize that in spite of the crises we endure, if we love the Lord, there is infinite joy to be had.

Whenever someone tells me they appreciate my service in Iraq, I can truly tell them it was a privilege for which I will be eternally grateful.

I can hardly wait for what the future brings.

A pilgrimage is a spiritual journey, and by definition, once the destination has been reached, the journey has ended.

My pilgrimage is far from over.

I've been asked, after my experience in Iraq, what do I plan to do now?

Where do I plan to go?

In 1936, B.B. McKinney was having dinner with a missionary friend, the Reverend R.S. Jones, who had recently returned from Brazil. The songwriter asked his friend that same question, and his response was the same as mine:

"Wherever He leads, I'll go."